Stalinist Russia

Series Editors

Heinemann Educational Publishers
Halley Court, Jordan Hill, Oxford, OX2 8EJ
a division of Reed Educational & Professional Publishing Ltd
Heinemann is a registered trademark of Reed Educational & Professional
Publishing Ltd

OXFORD MELBOURNE AUCKLAND
JOHANNESBURG BLANTYRE GABORONE
IBADAN PORTSMOUTH NH (USA) CHICAGO

First published 2000

ISBN 0 435 32720 8
04
10 9 8 7 6 5

Designed and typeset by Wyvern 21 Ltd

Printed and bound in Great Britain by CPI Bath

Photographic acknowledgements
The authors and publisher would like to thank the following for permission
to reproduce photographs: David King Collection: pp. 6, 14, 24, 31, 40,
43, 53, 57, 68, 81, 98, 103, 114, 124, 128: Hulton Getty: p. 36: Society
for Co-operation in Russian & Social Studies (SCRSS): pp. 5, 10, 27, 51,
59, 61.

Cover photograph: ©Peter Newark's Historical Pictures

Picture research by Elaine Willis

Acknowledgements from the author
I would like to thank the following for their help, advice and support
during the writing of this book: Nicholas Wilmott, Christine Bragg, Ian
Davies, my parents Margaret and Nigel Phillips with particular thanks to
Rosemary Rees and Nigel Kelly. I would also like to thank the many
students I have taught at Somerset College of Arts and Technology,
Worcester Technical College and Glan Afan Comprehensive School who
have given me so many ideas and so much inspiration.

CONTENTS

HOW TO USE THIS BOOK

This book is divided into distinct parts. 'The rise of Stalin 1924–9' and 'The Soviet Union 1928–41' are designed to meet the requirements of AS Level History. Both give an analytical narrative of events to explain what happened during this important period of Russian history. There are summary questions at the end of each chapter to challenge students to use the information in order to develop their skills in analysis and explanation and reinforce their understanding of the key issues. This part of the book will also provide a solid foundation in preparation for the more analytical work expected at A2 Level.

The A2 part of the book is more analytical in style. It contains interpretations of the key issues of this period and examines aspects of historiography central to the study of history at this level. These interpretations should be read in conjunction with the relevant AS chapter. In this way the student will be able to relate the information covered in the AS chapters to the more thematic and analytical interpretations in the A2 sections. The latter will also enable AS students to extend their understanding of the subject.

At the end of both AS and A2 parts there are assessment sections which have been designed to provide guidance on how students can meet the requirements of the new AS and A2 specifications provided by the three Awarding Bodies, Edexcel, AQA and OCR when answering questions.

It is hoped that the book will also be useful to general readers who wish to find their way around what is a sometimes complex but fascinating period of history.

AS SECTION: THE RISE OF STALIN 1924–29

INTRODUCTION

> ### Key questions
> - Why was Stalin able to emerge as leader of the Soviet Union by 1929?
> - How important were ideological differences in Stalin's rise to power?

Even before the death of Lenin, the leaders of the Bolshevik regime had begun to prepare themselves for the power struggle which was likely to occur when Lenin died. The main players in this battle were the members of the **Politburo**, the party's inner group of leaders, which in 1924 included Zinoviev, Kamenev, Tomsky, Bukharin, Rykov, Stalin and Trotsky. The Politburo was divided between those on the Right and those of the Left, a division largely over the pace of industrialisation. The key rivals, however, were Stalin and Trotsky.

When Lenin died in 1924 the Politburo was to provide a collective leadership but the period 1924 to 1929 was one of continuous struggle for power, which ultimately ended in the rise of Stalin to supreme leader of the Soviet Union. Trotsky was sent into internal exile before being expelled from the Soviet Union in 1928 and all of the leaders of the Left later met their deaths at Stalin's orders. The Right fared no better as arguments over the pace of industrialisation came to a head in 1927–28. As the Right was seen to threaten the progress of Stalin's economic plans, Stalin took action and was able to overcome his rivals.

New Politburo members were allies of Stalin such as Molotov and Kirov; usually men of limited ability but unlimited loyalty to Stalin. By the end of the 1920s Stalin was, therefore, in a powerful position and able to dominate the party leadership and launch his policies relatively unhindered.

CHAPTER 1

The rise of Stalin 1924–29

THE BOLSHEVIK REVOLUTION AT THE DEATH OF LENIN

In October 1917 the **Bolshevik Party** seized power during the chaos engulfing Russia following the fall of the Tsarist regime in February. The relatively small Bolshevik Party was helped in its successful overthrow of the Kerensky-led Provisional Government by the fact that Russia had fallen into confusion. For Lenin, the Bolshevik leader, holding on to power was a more difficult task. Yet despite attempts by counter-revolutionaries to remove them, the Bolsheviks were able to strengthen their position and introduce measures and reforms designed to bring about change based on the principles of socialism.

Lenin and the Bolsheviks believed in applying the principles developed by Karl Marx to the situation in Russia. Although the Bolsheviks had written at length about the evils of capitalism, their ideas on what to do when in power were rather vague. For Lenin it was necessary that the party govern on behalf of 'the people', by which he usually meant the proletariat (industrial workers), although sometimes he included the peasants. All land, factories and businesses (the 'means of production') had to be seized by the state in the name of 'the people' so that wealth and goods could be redistributed according to need. Eventually social classes would disappear as greater equality was achieved.

In practice, the Bolsheviks were faced with serious opposition that resulted in a bitter civil war. This situation forced the Bolsheviks into measures they had not foreseen. The scale of opposition resulted in widespread use of terror and short-term economic compromises, which had seen the return of some private industry under the New Economic Policy (NEP). These measures were seen as necessary in order to keep the Bolsheviks in power. Aspects of capitalism and its supporters were starting to reappear after 1921. The road to socialism was to be more difficult than the Bolshevik leadership had imagined. When Lenin died in 1924 the future of the revolution was uncertain. Lenin had given little firm indication of what should happen after his death. It was from this situation that **Stalin** rose as the sole leader of the Bolshevik Party and stamped his mark on the revolution.

Stalin: the young revolutionary

Stalin's background provides some clues as to the reasons behind his later actions. He was born in the southern state of Georgia, the son of a cobbler from peasant stock. His father ruled the family with violence and regular beatings may have hardened the young Stalin. His mother wanted him to become more than just a shoemaker and he was sent first to a church school and later to a theological seminary but instead of learning religious ideas, he became influenced by socialism and developed a deep sense of class hatred. 'Stalin', which meant man of steel, was an alias adopted by the young Joseph Djugashivili to help avoid detection by the Tsar's secret police as he undertook bank robberies to help finance the revolutionary movement. He was arrested six times between 1902 and 1913 for revolutionary activity. Stalin was exiled to Siberia, where the harsh conditions taught him the importance of being self-reliant. This characteristic was to become extremely useful during the struggle to gain the party leadership.

Stalin's efforts in the revolutionary cause had brought him to the attention of Lenin who was impressed by Stalin's organisational abilities and willingness to obey orders. As early as 1912 Stalin had become one of the six members of the Central Committee of the Bolshevik Party and he had helped to set up the party's newspaper *Pravda*. Lenin hoped Stalin would give the Central Committee more of a practical and working class image than the intellectuals who made up the majority of the party's leadership. As one of Lenin's most loyal followers, Stalin was rewarded with the position of Commissar for Nationalities after the October Revolution. However, Stalin's work in the Caucasus region drew Lenin's attention to some of Stalin's

Stalin, the young revolutionary (1900).

faults. Stalin had been rather heavy-handed in the dismissal of Georgian national representatives and Lenin was forced to intervene in order to resolve the situation. Thus, early in his career Stalin had shown most of the leading features of his character: he was an able and shrewd administrator with a tendency to ruthlessness. Stalin was not an intellectual or Marxist theorist, indeed his grasp of ideology was limited, but he was driven by a sense of class hatred stemming from his humble background and his experience of life in tsarist Russia. These characteristics were to be used to great effect in the struggle to succeed Lenin as leader of the **Communist Party**.

Stalin and Trotsky

When Lenin died in 1924 a collective leadership was formed: rule would be exercised by the Politburo rather than by one individual. Within this context Stalin was seen by many in the party as unlikely to establish himself as sole leader. To most members of the Communist Party in 1924 **Trotsky** was the most likely successor to Lenin. Trotsky

Leon Trotsky.

had taken a leading role in the October Revolution and during the civil war which occurred afterwards. It was Trotsky who seemed to be Lenin's 'right hand man'. Stalin, on the other hand, was seen as an administrator and a rather dull personality. It was easy to underestimate Stalin, a mistake the other members of the Politburo were to make.

If Stalin was to succeed Lenin as supreme leader of the Communist Party he would have to defeat Trotsky. Stalin and Trotsky were not just rivals for power, they were two very different personalities and their relationship was always strained. Trotsky had a formidable intellect and was a superb speaker, qualities Stalin was never to possess. Despite his brilliance Trotsky was unpopular with the party. He was from a wealthy Jewish background and his 'jewishness' did lead to some prejudice against him in the party. His intellectual background made him arrogant and

KEY TERM

Mensheviks In 1903 the Russian Social Democratic Labour Party split into two groups: the Mensheviks and the Bolsheviks. The Mensheviks were the more moderate group and, in terms of support, the largest of the two. Although both were committed to Marxist principles the split left a deep division.

those party members and opponents who came into conflict with Trotsky often found themselves at the sharp end of his wit and sarcasm. Trotsky had been a **Menshevik** until the summer of 1917 and his late conversion was seen as evidence of his lack of commitment to the party. He rarely attended party meetings and he did little to build up support for his position within the party. Many party members saw Trotsky as a danger to the revolution, someone who might betray it for his own ends. His connections with the Red Army, which he had organised during the civil war, gave the impression that Trotsky would use force to support and protect his own position. These concerns provided Stalin with a lot of material for undermining Trotsky's position.

The first major conflict between Stalin and Trotsky occurred when Stalin was appointed Commissar for Nationalities. In this position Stalin was involved in organising the Caucasus region during the civil war, including having some responsibility over military authority. This role brought him into conflict with Trotsky who was in charge of the Red Army. This seems to have been the start of their personal rivalry. This rivalry was to deepen when Lenin died in 1924.

Stalin's power base within the Communist Party

The uncertainty that arose after the death of Lenin worked to Stalin's advantage. Even before Lenin's death Stalin had laid the foundations for his rise to power. He had become **General Secretary** of the Party in 1922 and used the powers and influence of this position to gather information. Even Lenin's private home was bugged in order to keep Stalin supplied with information. Above all, Stalin recognised that the main focus of power was not the government but the party's Politburo. The growth in the scope and responsibility of the state had made some positions more important than others and as the party had developed into the various organs for administering the state it was the party structure which grew in power. The head of the party structure was the General Secretary and in 1924 it was Stalin who held this post.

Stalin had already gained useful information about the party and how it functioned before becoming General

KEY TERM

General Secretary This position was the head of the Party Secretariat, which was responsible for the day-to-day running of the party. The General Secretary co-ordinated work across all party departments and had access to a vast range of information which could be used to appoint local party officials. As the party organisation grew, so did the power and influence of the General Secretary.

Personalities: Stalin and Trotsky

Josef Stalin (1879–1953)

- from a peasant background
- deep sense of class hatred
- practically minded
- shrewd
- effective administrator
- ruthless and heavy handed

Leon Trotsky (1879–1940)

- from a wealthy, Jewish family background
- previously a Menshevik and his conversion to the Bolshevik cause was viewed by other Bolsheviks with suspicion
- formidable intellect
- appeared arrogant
- poor sense of judgement when dealing with other people
- unwilling to cultivate support within the Bolshevik Party
- preferred to work as an individual rather than as part of a team

Secretary. The positions of Commissar for Nationalities, Liaison Officer between the Politburo and the Orgburo (the party's bureau of organisation) and Head of the Workers' and Peasants' Inspectorate gave Stalin valuable experience. The key position, however, was that of General Secretary of the party, which Stalin gained in 1922. This post gave him access to over 26,000 personal files of party members – a useful source of information which could be used against rivals. In this post he had Dzerzhinsky, the head of the secret police, report to him regularly. There were few Politburo members not under his surveillance. More importantly, the post of General Secretary gave Stalin the right to appoint people to party positions and this provided him with a tool to promote his own supporters to key positions. As time went by more and

Stalin's positions in the party

People's Commissar for Nationalities (1917) In this post, held from 1917 until 1923, Stalin was in charge of the officials in the various republics outside Russia.

Liaison Officer between the Politburo and the Orgburo (1919) This post allowed Stalin to monitor party personnel and policy.

Head of the Workers' and Peasants' Inspectorate (1919) This was a wide-ranging post which involved the overseeing of the work of all government departments.

General Secretary of the Party (1922) This post gave Stalin access to personal files of party members and gave him the right to appoint his own supporters to positions as party officials.

more party officials owed their loyalty to Stalin. When it came to votes on party issues, Stalin could always outvote and outmanoeuvre his opponents. The power was in Stalin's hands.

KEY TERM

Lenin Enrolment
A campaign launched between 1923 and 1925 to increase the membership of the Bolshevik Party. It aimed to increase the number of industrial workers who were in the party.

Stalin's position was further enhanced by the launching of the '**Lenin Enrolment**' between 1923 and 1925. The aim of this membership drive was to increase the number of industrial workers in the party ranks. Over 500,000 workers were recruited, doubling the party's membership and this was to have important consequences. The new members were largely poorly educated and politically naïve. It is clear that these new members saw the party as a source of employment and of other privileges and that retaining these privileges depended on loyalty to those who had allowed them into the party. As General Secretary, it was Stalin who was responsible for supervising the 'Lenin Enrolment'. Stalin was always careful to ensure he could identify with the needs and demands of these new members and his humble background may well have helped him to do this.

Stalin and the 'Lenin legacy'

Stalin greatly enhanced his position within the Communist Party by attaching himself to the legacy of Lenin. With the rapid development of a cult of hero worship around Lenin this was a shrewd and highly effective policy.

On Lenin's death, Stalin moved quickly and gained the advantage of delivering the oration at Lenin's funeral. As a consequence of this Stalin was able to present himself as the chief mourner while Trotsky, on the other hand, did not attend the funeral. To many Party members this was seen as evidence of Stalin's intention to continue Lenin's work and Trotsky's lack of respect for Lenin's achievements. Stalin's position was also helped by Trotsky's refusal, along with other members of the Politburo, to publish Lenin's Testament. This document set out Lenin's views on each member of the Politburo with suggestions on how they should be used in the future. Of Stalin, Lenin had written 'he is too rude' and recommended his removal from the position of General Secretary. Unfortunately, Lenin was also critical of the other members of the Politburo and as a result the Testament was suppressed.

KEY CONCEPT

Lenin legacy A term used to describe the policies and ideas of Lenin after his death. Given the god-like status acquired by Lenin after 1924, it was seen as important and politically useful to protect the revolution as it had been inherited from Lenin.

Lenin lying in state, 1924.

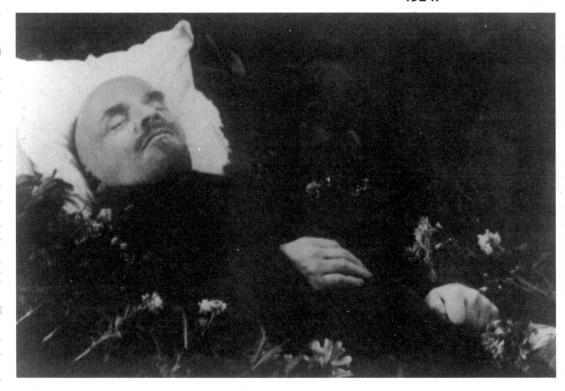

KEY TERM

'On Party Unity' This was the name given to a party rule which had been passed at the Tenth Party Congress in 1921. It banned the formation of factions within the party to ensure party solidarity was maintained. The sentence for anyone guilty of breaking this rule was the death penalty. The rule was a response to the opposition the party faced in 1921. In the struggle for power after Lenin's death this rule severely restricted those who wished to oppose the party line. As Stalin controlled the party organisation the rule tended to uphold his position.

KEY PEOPLE

Lev Kamenev (1883–1936)
Moderate by nature, Kamenev had been one of the founders of the Bolshevik Party. He had argued against the seizure of power in 1917. He had been chairman of the first Politburo and often acted as Lenin's deputy. After Lenin's death he sided with Stalin and Zinoviev against Trotsky but was outmanoeuvred by Stalin. He formed the 'United Opposition' with Trotsky and Zinoviev in 1926. He suffered the same fate as Zinoviev, being expelled from the party and executed in 1936.

Lenin's Testament

This was a document written by Lenin in December 1922; a postscript was added in January 1923. In it he set out his views on the way forward for the Bolshevik Revolution after his death. He used it to assess the strengths and weaknesses of each of the leading Bolsheviks and made comments on how they should be used in the future. Due to its critical content the document was not released when Lenin died in 1924.

At the funeral, Stalin was able to present himself as the heir to the **'Lenin legacy'**. Despite the objections of Krupskaya, Lenin's wife, it was decided that Lenin's body would be embalmed. The decision may well have been Stalin's; if not, he certainly approved of it. Lenin quickly became an almost god-like figure to the party and to present oneself as the worthy continuer of the Lenin legacy was a formidable claim to power. As Stalin seemed to have few ideas of his own, his promise to apply those of Lenin seemed all the more convincing. Trotsky, on the other hand, completely misjudged this mood and launched an attack on Lenin's policies.

The defeat of Trotsky and the Left

In 1924 Trotsky launched an attack on the growth of the party bureaucracy. He highlighted the danger of the bureaucracy becoming a class in itself, which would work for its own benefit. Trotsky's criticisms of the bureaucracy were unpopular in the party, and consequently Stalin was able to effectively isolate Trotsky by working with **Zinoviev** and **Kamenev**. One factor in his favour was Lenin's rule against factionalism, *On Party Unity*. This had been issued in the aftermath of the Kronstadt Mutiny of 1921 when the party had faced serious opposition. It condemned the forming of factions in the party and may well have limited Trotsky's attempts to organise his supporters; he would have been aware that the accusation of factionalism was a serious charge which carried the death penalty. Stalin could always use the accusation of factionalism to frustrate opposition within the party. It was a weapon he was to use to good effect against his opponents when differences arose over ideology and policy.

In 1926 Trotsky joined forces with Zinoviev and Kamenev to form the 'United Opposition'. This was a grouping of the Left of the party. The views of the Left concerned the future of the New Economic Policy (NEP). When Lenin introduced the NEP in 1921 he made it clear that it was to be a temporary measure, designed to get the economy moving again after the disruption caused by the civil war. Lenin felt that in order to bring about economic recovery a compromise with the peasantry was needed, as was the return of small-scale industry to private hands. Lenin gave no indication of how long this temporary measure should last. To the Left, the NEP, with its elements of capitalist free enterprise, was seen as a betrayal of the aims of the Revolution. It allowed the peasants to sell surplus foodstuffs at market for a profit and this, according to the Left, was holding back the move to socialism. The Right, on the other hand, saw the NEP as a legitimate policy which should be retained providing it worked; in other words, so long as enough food was produced to meet the population's needs.

Trotsky was also concerned about the issue of 'Permanent Revolution'. The priority, according to Trotsky, was the need to spread worldwide revolution, otherwise the success of the Bolshevik Revolution in Russia would not be guaranteed. The idea of Permanent Revolution led to division in 1925 when Stalin decided to make his mark on policy direction by promoting the idea of 'Socialism in One Country'. This called for a strengthening of the Bolshevik Revolution through the economic modernisation of the Soviet Union using its own industrial resources. This implied a different emphasis to that of Trotsky and provoked an attack by Trotsky on Stalin's policy.

The United Opposition was always a wary alliance of different personalities, making it easy for Stalin to exploit their differences and, as General Secretary, he was in a position to deliver the votes from his own supporters in the Party to defeat them. Although the United Opposition was

KEY PEOPLE

Grigory Zinoviev (1883–1936) A leading member of the Left wing of the party. Zinoviev was a volatile personality, subject to mood swings. He found Stalin difficult to deal with. Stalin used Zinoviev and Kamenev to form a Triumvirate against Trotsky but after Trotsky's defeat Stalin turned against them. In 1926 Zinoviev joined the 'United Opposition' (with Trotsky and Kamenev) but was demoted from the Politburo and expelled from the party in 1927. After publicly admitting to mistakes and praising Stalin, Zinoviev was readmitted to the party before being expelled again in 1932. He was tried before a show trial in 1936 for crimes against the state and executed.

KEY TERM

United Opposition This was the alliance formed in 1926 by those on the Left of the party: Trotsky, Zinoviev and Kamenev. The United Opposition was formed to oppose the continuation of the NEP. As Trotsky had been a former enemy of Zinoviev and Kamenev it was a strange alliance that lacked conviction. By this time all three leaders of the United Opposition were seen as outsiders and Stalin was able to use the party machinery to defeat them. Accused of factionalism, they were expelled from the party.

'Permanent Revolution' versus 'Socialism in One Country'

- **Permanent Revolution** This was the name of the policy vigorously promoted by Trotsky, which saw the need to spread world revolution as the priority after the Bolshevik Revolution of 1917. Trotsky argued that without world revolution the revolution in Russia would not survive.

- **Socialism in One Country** This was the name given to the policy promoted by Stalin in the 1920s, which saw the strengthening of the revolution within Russia as more important than spreading revolution abroad.

KEY TERMS

The New Economic Policy (NEP) was introduced by Lenin in 1921 to reduce opposition to the Bolshevik regime and to help restart the economy after the civil war. The NEP allowed the return of small-scale industries to private ownership and introduced incentives into government-owned industries. It also put an end to the forcible taking of grain from the peasants.

The Right Opposition This group consisted of people in the party who wished to see the continuation of the NEP rather than Stalin's forced industrialisation of the USSR under the first Five-Year Plan. Its leaders were Bukharin, Rykov and Tomsky. By 1930 they had been removed from their positions of power in the party. The Right Opposition was finally dealt with by the purges in 1938: most of its members were executed.

able to present their arguments at a Central Committee meeting in 1926 they were defeated and at the Fifteenth Party Conference, later in the same year, they were not allowed to speak. From this point onwards they had to work in secret. Accused of forming factions, they were expelled from the Politburo and either demoted or sent into internal exile. Zinoviev and Kamenev were allowed to stay in the party after renouncing their previous views but Trotsky preferred to stick to his principles and was exiled to Alma-Ata in Central Asia.

The defeat of the Right

The defeat of the Left raised the political temperature and in the winter of 1927–28 the party leadership found itself once again divided over the issue of industrialisation as Stalin aimed to launch the first Five-Year Plan to stimulate the economy. The disagreement was over when and how industrialisation should take place. All of the Bolshevik leadership saw industrialisation as a necessary part of the consolidation of socialism and with it the Communist Party itself but divisions occurred over the best way to achieve this. In order to industrialise, more food would be needed to support the growth of urban and industrial workers. The Left had seen the use of force as the only way to make the peasants grow more food. The Right preferred a policy of persuasion, arguing that the use of force could actually cause food production to decline because of opposition from the peasantry. In early 1928, the proposals for the Five-Year Plan led to the emergence of a **Right Opposition** group which argued the case for a continuation of the NEP and opposed the policy of rapid industrialisation under the plan. The leaders of the Right in the Politburo were **Tomsky**, **Rykov**, and **Bukharin**.

In this debate Stalin saw the views of the Right as standing in the way of his policy of 'Socialism in One Country', threatening to slow down any progress that could be made in strengthening the economic base of the Soviet Union and socialism. After the removal of the threat from the Left it seemed that Stalin was prepared to adopt their ideas of

Nikolai Bukharin (1888–1938) A leading economic theorist who was very much on the Left of the party until the NEP, he became strongly opposed to the forced industrialisation of the Soviet Union and was one of the most vocal in support of the continuation of the NEP. When Stalin became convinced that the NEP must go, Bukharin's position was under threat. Bukharin refused to build up a power base in the party due to a sense of loyalty and as a result he was in a weak position. He was removed from the Politburo in 1929 but continued to support the Right Opposition. He was executed during the purges of 1938.

A 1927 cartoon ridiculing the United Opposition. Trotsky is the organ-grinder; Zinoviev is the singer, and Kamenev is the parrot.

KEY PEOPLE

Alexei Rykov (1881–1938)
Rykov became Head of the
Government on the death of
Lenin and was an ally of
Stalin against Trotsky. A
leading member of the Right
in the party over the issue of
the NEP. Rykov was strongly
in favour of the NEP's
retention. When Stalin
decided to end the NEP
Rykov's position was
threatened. He was dismissed
as Head of the Government
by Stalin in 1930. Arrested in
1937 for allegedly planning
to assassinate Stalin, he was
executed in 1938.

**Mikhail Tomsky
(1880–1936)** A trade
unionist who was on the
Right of the party. He
supported Bukharin in the
debate over the NEP and as a
result fell out with Stalin in
1930. He was removed from
the Politburo but continued
to fight for trade union rights.
He was due to be put on trial
with Bukharin and Rykov but
committed suicide in 1936.

rapid industrialisation by abandoning the NEP. Stalin used
his power and influence in the party to ensure the Right
was defeated in votes over policy decisions. By early 1929
the members of the Right Opposition in the Politburo
were identified by name and all were removed from their
posts except Rykov, who remained Head of the
Government until 1930.

Stalin had defeated the Right and the Left opposition
groups within the party. The collective leadership, which
had been declared in 1924 at the death of Lenin, was no
more. Stalin had whittled away at the power and positions
of his main rivals until, by early 1929, he was in a
dominant position. He was now free to implement his
policies of industrialisation and collectivisation under the
Five-Year Plan without opposition.

SUMMARY QUESTIONS

1 What positions did Stalin hold in the Bolshevik Party
between 1917 and 1924. How did they increase his
power and influence?

2 What is meant by the 'Lenin legacy' and how did Stalin
use it to his own advantage?

3 Explain the difference between 'Permanent Revolution'
and 'Socialism in One Country'.

4 How did the Right and Left of the Bolshevik Party
disagree over the future of the NEP in the 1920s?

AS SECTION: THE SOVIET UNION 1928–41

INTRODUCTION

> **Key questions**
> - Why did Stalin launch the Five-Year Plans and collectivisation?
> - What were the results of Stalin's economic policies between 1928 and 1941?
> - Why did Stalin launch the Great Purges of the 1930s?
> - What degree of social change was brought about by the Soviet government between 1928 and 1941?
> - What changes were there in the ways in which the Soviet government used popular culture and the arts between 1928 and 1941?

The period 1928 to 1941 was one of enormous change. It saw the implementation of the Five-Year Plans, collectivisation and a wave of terror. These policies were closely associated with Stalin to the extent that historians have referred to them collectively as 'Stalinism'. Although the role of Stalin has been a subject of debate, these policies brought about fundamental change in the Soviet Union under what is often termed 'Stalin's Revolution'.

The Five-Year Plans involved an extension of state control over all aspects of the economy as the country pushed forward with large-scale industrialisation. Industrialisation was accompanied by urbanisation and both needed to be supported by greater production of food. The industrialisation programme was therefore linked to the implementation of a policy of collectivisation in agriculture. Not only would collectivisation increase food production but it would also strengthen the revolution by ridding the country of those seen as class enemies. The overriding objective of these economic policies was to turn the Soviet Union into a modern industrial country able to withstand an attack by the capitalist powers.

The results of Stalin's economic policies were mixed: the industrial base was undoubtedly strengthened but not all sectors of the economy flourished. Both the pace of industrialisation and the policy of collectivisation led to criticisms of Stalin's policies and opposition developed both within and outside of the party. The Soviet Union became a state under siege desperate to defend itself not only from the enemy outside – the capitalist powers – but also from the enemy within. In the 1930s the enemy within was identified and dealt with by a series of purges known as the Great Terror. Enemies of the state were tried and executed, including such well-known names as Zinoviev, Kamenev and Bukharin. The use of terror, alongside the widespread economic changes taking place, brought about significant changes in society and by 1941 the communist government was firmly established with Stalin at its head. The Soviet Union had made a significant advance towards becoming a world industrial power but it had been achieved at a great cost in terms of human lives.

CHAPTER 2

The Five-Year Plans

One of the central aims of the communist regime in the Soviet Union was to industrialise the country. The Soviet economy had made advances under Lenin's NEP but economically, the Soviet Union remained behind the rest of Europe. The **Five-Year Plans** were designed to break away from the NEP, with its capitalist elements, and bring about rapid industrialisation to modernise the economy and bring about **socialism**. The changes introduced under the plans were to transform the USSR from a backward peasant-based country into a modern, urban and industrial-based society.

WHY DID STALIN LAUNCH THE FIVE-YEAR PLANS?

The fear of foreign invasion

The decision to launch the first Five-Year Plan in 1928 was based on a combination of economic and political factors which were linked by a fear of foreign invasion. Despite the economic progress made under the NEP the Soviet economy was still backward when compared to the rest of Europe. In the 1920s the Soviet Union was still producing less coal and steel than France. If the Soviet Union was ever to face an attack from the capitalist powers it would need a much stronger industrial base. Memories of the help given by Britain, France, the US and Japan to the Whites during the civil war of 1918–21 seemed to confirm suspicions that the West would wish to invade and destroy communism at some point in the future. These fears came to the surface in 1927 when a series of events were seen as evidence of an impending attack on the Soviet Union. In 1927 there was a raid by the British government on the Soviet trade mission in London; in China, communists were attacked by the Kuomintang forces of Chiang Kai Shek; and a Soviet diplomat was assassinated in Poland. The Soviet government presented these events as evidence of an anti-Soviet conspiracy. In these circumstances it was

KEY TERMS

Five-Year Plans
Government plans for the implementation of economic policies. Under Stalin these were aimed at the rapid industrialisation of the Soviet Union. The first Five-Year Plan ran from 1928 to 1932. The emphasis was on heavy industry in a state-owned and state-directed economy and as a result private businesses and trade were to be swept away.

easy to argue that if the Soviet Union was to survive it would need to be put on a war footing. As Stalin stated in 1931: 'We are 50 to 100 years behind the advanced countries. We must make good this distance in 10 years. Either we do it or we shall be crushed'. Industrialisation was seen as essential to ensure Soviet victory in an impending war. Thus, to industrialise was patriotic and this formed an important part of Stalin's cry of 'Socialism in One Country'. The chaos caused in Germany by the Wall Street Crash of 1929 and the subsequent rise of Hitler with his strident anti-communist statements provided a further incentive for the successful completion of the Five-Year Plans as the 1930s wore on.

Economic reasons

Fear of invasion gave added weight to the economic reasons used to justify the Five-Year Plans. Under the NEP industrial production, although improving, remained disappointing to many in the Communist Party. By 1926 pre-war levels of production had been reached in many sectors but production was nowhere near what it could have been. The disruption of the First World War and the civil war had damaged Russia's industrial infrastructure, and essential services such as distribution remained haphazard. Soviet production figures were still far below the modern industrial economies of Western Europe. State control under the Five-Year Plan would enable the government to direct the economy and ensure the adequate production and distribution of essential materials including the food needed to support industrial and urban growth. With government direction and control the economic resources of the Soviet Union could be maximised. Since the communist takeover in 1917, trade with the rest of the world had been severely reduced. The Soviet Union would have to rely on its own resources. State control would ensure that the full potential of these resources would be realised, so as to to bring about rapid industrialisation.

Political reasons

Although there was an economic case for the Five-Year Plan this was secondary to political reasons. To all Communist Party members industrialisation was seen as a necessary development in order to ensure the survival of

Class enemies A term used to describe those groups in society who were seen as remnants of the old capitalist society. They included:

Kulaks Peasants who owned their own farm and as a result tended to be strongly opposed to collectivisation. The term 'kulak' literally meant 'tightfisted'.

Nepmen Originally a term of abuse used by communists to describe those private business people and traders who had gained under the NEP.

Bourgeois experts A term used by Bolsheviks to describe former managers and owners of industry who were given jobs after nationalisation because they possessed skills and expertise which were desperately needed. The 'bourgeois experts' were resented by many industrial workers because few of them were Bolsheviks yet they retained positions of importance.

the revolution. It was believed that socialism, and with it the Communist Party, would not survive in a non-industrial society. It was therefore essential to undertake a programme of industrial development. Industrialisation would create many more members of the **proletariat**, the backbone of the revolution. Industrialisation was therefore seen as a form of social engineering. The Five-Year Plan, with its large-scale nationalisation and state control would get rid of the detested **Nepmen**, those private business owners and traders who survived under the NEP. As people who made a profit from their trade, the Nepmen were seen as capitalists, **class enemies** who presented a reminder of the old world and its values. How could socialism survive, it was argued, with the enemy lurking within? These capitalist elements concerned with selfish gains needed to be wiped out and the Five-Year Plan would achieve this.

What was the role of Stalin in the decision to launch the Five-Year Plan?

It is tempting to see Stalin adopting these policies in order to strengthen his own personal power as undisputed leader of the Soviet Union. After getting rid of Trotsky and the Left of the party he could adopt their ideas on industrialisation without compromising his own position. Indeed, after the Left had been neutralised the Right was in a stronger position but they too could be sidelined if the NEP was abandoned. The Right, led by Politburo members Bukharin, Tomsky and Rykov, were in favour of keeping the NEP, arguing that the forcing of peasants on to collectives would actually lead to a decline in food production. By 1928 Stalin argued that the NEP should go because, as a compromise with the peasantry, it was holding back the industrialisation of the Soviet Union. The launching of the Five-Year Plan saw the effective removal of the leaders of the Right in early 1929 as well as the extension of the state, through party-controlled planning agencies. It was thus instrumental in Stalin's increase in power. This view of Stalin's motives for abandoning the NEP presents Stalin as a scheming opportunist interested above all in personal power. This appears to be an overly cynical viewpoint. The influence of the Right in the party is difficult to gauge but it seems unlikely that they posed a serious threat to Stalin. It is also much more likely that Stalin was articulating the views of the majority of party members. Rather than working for merely personal motives, Stalin was also reacting to pressure from the rank and file of the party membership.

The attitudes of rank and file communists

Although the launching of the Five-Year Plan has been seen as a 'revolution from above' it was also, to a large extent, a 'revolution from below'. The attitudes of rank and file communists were pushing Stalin towards large-scale industrialisation. As the 1920s wore on many rank and file Communist Party members became disillusioned with the revolution. The targets of their frustration were the so-called class enemies who had survived the revolution and whose position was strengthened by the compromises of the NEP. The Nepmen, **kulaks** and '**bourgeois experts**' were seen as reminders of the old world that had not been swept away. Many rank and file party members harked back to the 'good old days' of the civil war when there seemed to be something worth fighting for. This dissatisfaction was building up in the party and Stalin saw the potential of aligning himself with these views in order to strengthen his own position. Rapid industrialisation would provide the opportunity to sweep away the remnants of the old system, move to a more socialist framework and placate the rank and file. The policy drive was couched in the terminology of war to appeal to those who had fought in the civil war. The strength of these attitudes became apparent when the Five-Year Plan was implemented. It was often the case that local party officials applied the new policies on the ground with more force than the government had intended. Thus, Stalin's drive for rapid industrialisation and collectivisation was popular with the party membership, securing support for Stalin's position as supreme leader of the Soviet Union.

There is no doubt that the policies of the Five-Year Plans strengthened the personal power of Stalin and enabled him to extend his control over both the party and the country but they were also measures which were popular with the rank and file of the party. Stalin's decision to launch these policies was based on a need to ensure the survival of the

KEY TERM

Rank and file communists
All members of the Communist Party other than the leaders.

KEY CONCEPTS

Revolution from above
Change that is driven by those who already hold power.

Revolution from below
Change that is driven by those who do not hold power, such as the masses.

revolution; a decision which would benefit not just party members but also the party leader.

THE IMPLEMENTATION OF THE FIVE-YEAR PLANS

The abandonment of the NEP and the introduction of the push towards rapid industrialisation was made in 1928. Industrialisation was to be directed by **Gosplan**, the State Planning Authority. Targets were set for those industries which the government saw as having priority in terms of modernisation and resources were allocated accordingly. **The first Five-Year Plan** (1928–32) concentrated on heavy industry, such as coal, steel and iron, using the ideas of **Preobrazhensky**, the economist theorist, although Stalin did not acknowledge this. Consumer industries, such as textiles and household goods, were neglected. The focus on heavy industry was a consequence that the Soviet Union had to live with for the rest of its history. The original justification for this focus was the need to build up an industrial infrastructure of factories, plant and communications before other sectors could flourish. This was a reasonable justification for the first Five-Year Plan and **the second Plan of 1933–37** initially did set higher targets for the production of consumer goods but as the 1930s progressed, the rise of Hitler in Germany changed the focus towards the needs of defence, which meant that heavy industry continued to receive priority. **The third Five-Year Plan**, launched in 1938, was geared even more directly towards arms production in order to meet the threat of Germany.

WHAT WERE THE RESULTS OF STALIN'S FIVE-YEAR PLANS 1928–41?

The targets of the first Five-Year Plan of 1928–32 were very ambitious to start with, but as the plan was put into effect they were constantly raised to unrealistic heights. It was, as McCauley (1993) puts it, 'as if mathematics had ceased to function'. The goal became not just fulfilling the plan but over-fulfilling it. Not to do so became a sign of a lack of commitment towards the revolution. Although targets were rarely reached, the achievements of the Five-Year Plans were impressive and transformed the Soviet Union into a major industrial power with a modern, if unbalanced, economy.

Industrial expansion under the first Five-Year Plan was largely the result of making more efficient use of existing factories and equipment. New plants were built but they did not make a significant impact on production until after 1934. Large industrial centres such as Magnitogorsk and Gorki were built from scratch and became large cities.

KEY CONCEPT

New industrial centres
Under the second Five-Year Plan (1933–37) there was a policy of concentrating new industry in large centres. Magnitogorsk and Gorki were examples of massive new industrial complexes built during this period.
Magnitogorsk, in southwest Siberia, was based on the metal industries, especially iron and steel. The town was built from scratch and workers were encouraged to move to the site. In 1929 there were only 25 people living at Magnitogorsk; three years later this number had increased to 250,000. In the early years of construction, living conditions for workers were poor and many lived in huts or tents. The locals referred to the site as 'Shanghai'. Despite its conditions the city experienced enormous growth and was seen as one of the successes of the Five-Year Plans.

Magnitogorsk, the vast industrial city of the Five-Year Plans.

Facilities at these centres were primitive, with workers housed in tents and temporary huts. The material rewards were limited and work was hard. The workers who often volunteered to move to these sites had to rely on their revolutionary attitudes and socialist beliefs for motivation. Many sites had statues to Lenin built in order to inspire the workers to greater revolutionary achievements.

Industry was located in the remoter areas of the USSR such as Kazakhstan, and there was a deliberate policy of locating East of the Ural Mountains, where industry would be safer against an attack from the west.

The second Five-Year Plan drew on lessons learnt from the chaotic planning of the first plan and made more use of technical expertise and with the new industrial centres starting production the results were impressive. In particular, coal production rose substantially during the second plan. The chemical industry also made progress but the oil industry remained disappointing. The third plan became heavily focused on the defence industry in the light of international tension.

Overall, the period of 1928 to 1941 saw a four-fold increase in the production of steel and a six-fold increase in coal production. There was substantial progress made in the production of energy, iron ore and metal industries, but consumer industries suffered. The production of textiles actually declined during the first Five-Year Plan and the housing industry was virtually ignored. The shortage of consumer goods was made worse by the fact that collectivisation had destroyed a lot of cottage industry previously undertaken in rural areas.

Official Soviet production in the years 1927 to 1937 (Taken from A Nove, 'An Economic History of the USSR', 1992)

	1927 Actual	1932 Actual	1932 Goal	1937 Actual	1937 Goal
Wool cloth (million metres)	97.0	93.3	270.0	108.3	226.6
Coal (million tons)	35.4	64.3	75.0	128.0	152.5
Oil (million tons)	11.7	21.4	22.0	28.5	46.8
Electricity (100m kwh)	5.0	13.4	22.0	36.2	38.0
Pig iron (million tons)	3.3	6.2	10.0	14.5	16.0
Steel (million tons)	4.0	5.9	10.4	17.7	17.0

The economic results of the industrialisation programme were achieved at the expense of the social conditions of the workers. In the pressure to meet the targets set by the Five-Year Plans, safety was neglected and working conditions worsened. Machinery was used without proper training or protection. Levels of pay were low although factory shops did provide some goods at reasonable prices. The government ordered factory canteens to keep rabbits to ensure a supply of food. One consequence of worsening conditions was that workers became difficult to keep, until the passport system which restricted the movement of workers was introduced in 1932. Increased absenteeism was another sign of discontent and it became such a problem that in 1939 it was made a criminal offence which could result in imprisonment. Of course, with labour being in such short supply these measures were not always applied. Slave labour from the labour camps had to be used to meet the need for workers. To encourage workers to work harder, incentives were introduced: Soviet workers were encouraged to work like the hero **Stakhanov**, a coalminer from the Donbass region who mined, in one shift, fifteen times the average amount of coal; there were rewards for model workers, such as a new flat or bigger rations; slackers were held up to ridicule.

The Five-Year Plans also had an impact on society as a whole, as they resulted in a huge growth in the industrial proletariat, which grew by 38 per cent between 1926 and 1933. Economic planning was partly social engineering for political reasons. With a more urban-based society the position of socialism, and with it the Communist Party, was strengthened. The Five-Year Plans saw the rapid extension of the state's power over the economy. People's Commissariats were set up to coordinate the differing branches of industry and party officials were used at factory level to ensure orders from the centre were carried out. Yet factory managers were not merely obedient servants of the centre. The pressure to fulfil increasingly unrealistic targets led them to use a wide range of enterprising methods which included, on occasions, ambushing resources destined for other factories. Bribery was another useful tool of the factory manager. The corruption for which the

Alexei Stakhanov 1906–77
A coal miner from the Donbass region who apparently mined fifteen times as much coal as the average miner in one shift. He was used as the model worker for others to follow. He toured the country encouraging his fellow workers to follow his example. The Soviet leadership used him to attack industrial management who seemed unable to meet the high targets set under the Five-Year Plans. In the 1980s it was revealed that Stakhanov's achievement had been a fraud: he had been helped by a team of support workers.

A statue of Alexei Stakhanov, the model Soviet worker of the 1930s.

USSR became infamous had its roots in the policy requirements of the 1930s.

The Five-Year Plans saw a drive against the Nepmen as small businesses and shopkeepers were often forced to join state co-operatives. As the state took over nearly all of the urban economy, it became clear that the mixed economy of the NEP was at an end. Within the factories there was a concerted campaign against the so-called 'bourgeois

Summary of results of Five-Year Plans

Economic
- emphasis on heavy industry
- six-fold increase in coal production
- four-fold increase in steel production
- chaotic implementation and increased corruption
- building of large industrial centres
- neglect of consumer industries
- decline in textile production

Social
- decline in working conditions – e.g. safety measures
- low levels of pay
- worker discontent at poor conditions
- introduction of passport system to prevent workers leaving jobs
- use of slave labour to overcome labour shortages
- huge growth in the number of industrial workers

Political
- control of the Communist Party strengthened through the organisation of industrial workers
- capitalist classes removed – e.g. Nepmen and 'bourgeois experts'
- expansion of government's role in the economy through central planning
- strengthening of Stalin's position as those opposed to the Five-Year Plans were removed

experts', those technical staff who had kept their positions because the state needed their expertise to keep industry running smoothly. This policy, directed by the government, built on the prejudices of the industrial workers and rank and file communists and was probably encouraged by the experts' belief that the targets of the Five-Year Plan could never be achieved. The removal of the 'bourgeois experts' would open up job opportunities to more loyal, if less trained, communist members. In 1928 there were a series of show trials against 'bourgeois expe accused of 'wrecking' and deliberate sabotage, often in collaboration with foreign agents. As class enemies, this group was seen as the enemy within, and could not be tolerated. Thus, another part of the old world was to disappear and in its place socialism would be stronger. Unfortunately, the loss of this group of technical experts slowed the economic progress made under the Five-Year Plans.

CONCLUSION

Between 1941 and 1945 the Soviet Union showed that it was able to defend itself against an attack by Nazi Germany and defeat the invading forces. On the face of it, this seemed to prove that Stalin's aim of transforming the USSR into a modern industrial society able to withstand attack by foreign capitalist powers had been achieved. The Soviet Union had undoubtedly made enormous economic progress but beneath the surface this progress was unbalanced, with a marked decline in certain sectors while others showed impressive growth. Economic progress was often achieved amid, and in spite of, chaos in planning and application of policy and at an enormous human cost. The Five-Year Plans had transformed the economy and society of the Soviet Union and, in doing so, greatly increased the power and influence of the Communist Party and of Stalin, as leader of the Soviet Union.

SUMMARY QUESTIONS

1 Why did Stalin launch the Five-Year Plans?

2 Why were many new industrial centres, such as Magnitogorsk, built east of the Urals?

3 Why did Alexei Stakhanov become famous in the 1930s?

4 What impact had the Five-Year Plans had on the Soviet economy by 1941?

CHAPTER 3

Collectivisation

Widespread changes in agriculture accompanied Stalin's policy of industrialisation. The Five-Year Plans included the policy of **collectivisation**. The industrialisation intended under the Five-Year Plans was to be supported by food surpluses generated by changing the basis of farming in the countryside. It was a policy which had fundamental consequences for the rural population of the Soviet Union.

WHAT WERE THE REASONS FOR COLLECTIVISATION?

The NEP, introduced by Lenin in 1921, had left agriculture largely unchanged since the revolution of 1917. It had been a compromise with the peasantry over the issue of government control of food supplies. As a result, by 1928 agriculture in the Soviet Union was still run largely on an individual basis by peasant households under the supervision of the **mir**, a body made up of village elders. By 1928 both economic and political forces were pushing Stalin towards abandoning the NEP and forcing the peasants into the collectivisation of farming.

The link with industry

A fear of invasion by foreign powers had convinced many in the Communist Party that there was an urgent need to industrialise. A modern economic base was seen as essential if the Soviet Union was to defend itself against an attack by the capitalist powers. Yet industrial development would be possible only if it was supported by an increase in agricultural productivity. Industrialisation would lead to an increase in the population of towns and cities, a population that would need to be fed by an increase in food supply. The new industries could also require some technology from abroad and the Soviet Union would therefore need a source of foreign exchange to pay for this. The government needed food surpluses to export in order to get foreign

Tractors arriving at a collective, 1933.

exchange. Yet agriculture would have to provide more than just food to support industry. Labour would be needed in the new industrial centres and this could be achieved in the short-term only by the mechanisation of agriculture. This would enable labourers to be released from the countryside to work in industry. Thus, the policy of industrialisation could be achieved only if agriculture was made more efficient.

In 1928 arguments in the party over agricultural production came to a head. Stalin had become convinced that the state of agriculture and the attitudes of sections of the peasantry were holding back industrial progress. **State procurements** – the amount of surplus grain given to the government by the peasants – had been falling since 1926. The peasants had become wary of growing too much food, knowing it would be seized by the state at a low price. This acted as a disincentive to raise production, as did the lack of industrial goods available to buy with any profit made from a food surplus. The problem for the government was that industrial production could be increased only if food production rose. This problem, known as the 'scissors crisis', provided the government with its central economic dilemma. Stalin saw the solution as a forced policy of collectivisation to raise food production.

Economic factors

Agriculture, centred on small peasant plots, was very inefficient compared with the rest of Europe. Most farms were owned by peasant households with their land distributed in a piecemeal fashion. The creation of collective farms where peasants would be grouped together in larger farm units would create economies of scale. Hedgerows and boundaries could be ripped out and the resulting larger units would make the use of machinery more viable and cost-effective. The use of machinery would enable food production to be increased and reduce the labour requirements of agricultural production. This would release many much-needed workers for the growing industrial plants.

Soviet agriculture in 1928

- based on small peasant plots
- little use of machinery
- largely privately owned by peasants, some of whom were referred to as kulaks, or 'richer' peasants
- very few collective farms: the government's attempt to collectivise had been dropped with the NEP
- agriculture controlled at local level by the mir, made up of village elders
- inefficient, especially when compared with the rest of Europe
- unable to produce enough surplus grain to support further industrial and urban growth

Political factors

As well as improving the efficiency of agriculture, collectivisation would help extend socialism to the countryside and therefore ensure the survival of the revolution. The Bolsheviks had introduced the Land Decree in 1917 to take large landed estates from the aristocracy but they had never intended that land should be the personal property of individual peasants. The NEP had put aside attempts to collectivise the peasants and by 1925 less than one per cent of farmland was collectivised. In this situation the principle of private ownership was maintained in the minds of the peasants and some used the compromises introduced under the NEP to make a profit. Collectivisation provided the opportunity for getting rid of the kulaks, those richer peasants who seemed to benefit from the NEP. In the eyes of the communists, the kulaks hoarded food for their own consumption rather than providing it for industrial workers in the towns. This led to pressure on the government leadership to rid the country of this capitalist class. To fail to do so would hold back the progress towards socialism.

The role of Stalin in the launching of collectivisation

Many rank and file communists put pressure on the leadership to abandon the NEP and introduce collectivisation in the spirit of waging a war against the enemies of socialism. Stalin aligned himself with these views but the policy of collectivisation also allowed him to rid the party leadership of the Right; those who had been in favour of the NEP. Thus, the decision to collectivise, like that of the Five-Year Plans, was aimed at increasing his own position and power at the expense of others within the leadership. Those, such as Bukharin, Tomsky and Rykov, who argued in favour of the NEP were demoted within the party.

Collectivisation was seen by Stalin and many in the Communist Party as both an economic and political necessity. It would sweep away the remaining elements of capitalism in the countryside and enable rapid industrialisation to take place. This would ensure the Soviet Union was modernised in order to defeat the threats to the revolution from both inside and outside the country and also safeguard its survival. In doing so, Stalin's position as well as that of the party, would be strengthened.

WHAT WERE THE RESULTS OF COLLECTIVISATION?

Initially the process of collectivisation was to be undertaken on a voluntary basis, but by the autumn of 1929 coercion was being used to quicken the pace. In this all-out drive for collectivisation the kulaks were not to be admitted to the new collectives. Labelled as 'class enemies' they were to be deported to Siberia and the Urals. The process of collectivisation involved local party officials going into villages and announcing the organisation of a collective farm (**kolkhoz**) and lecturing the peasants on the advantages of forming a collective until enough of them had signed up as members. The collective could then seize animals, grain supplies and buildings in the village as the property of the collective. The term 'kulak' was applied not just to the richer peasants but to any peasant who refused to join.

The implementation of collectivisation led to violent opposition from a large number of peasants, particularly in the richer agricultural areas of the Ukraine and the Caucasus region. Rather than hand over their property to the state many kulaks set fire to their farms and slaughtered their animals. Party officials were sometimes murdered on arrival in the villages. The regime dealt with this opposition by sending in **dekulakisation squads** – party members from the cities – to help forcefully organise collectives. The **OGPU**, the secret police, were also used to round up kulaks and other peasants who refused to co-operate and they were deported to remote regions of the USSR, often to labour camps. On some occasions the Red Army was used to quell unrest in the countryside; some troublesome villages were bombed out of existence by the air force.

The peasants' opposition resulted in a temporary backdown by Stalin, who in March 1930 issued his article 'Dizzy with Success' blaming over-zealous local party officials for 'excesses'. Yet this slowdown in the process of collectivisation lasted only long enough to ensure that the

Kolkhoz A collective farm.

Dekulakisation squads
Groups of loyal party members who were sent into the countryside to force the peasants into collectives. In this way the kulaks would be eliminated. In practice 'dekulakisation' covered a range of methods for eliminating the kulaks, including murder.

OGPU The official name of the secret police from 1922 until 1934, when it was replaced by the NKVD.

peasants sowed the new year's crop. Some concessions were offered to the peasantry. Members of the collectives could have some animals and a small garden plot for their own use but the programme of collectivisation continued to be pursued. By 1932 62 per cent of peasant households had been collectivised, rising to 93 per cent in 1937.

The effect of collectivisation on the village was substantial. The reorganisation into collectives provided an opportunity to remove other elements of the old world such as the village priest and the school master. In 1930 the mir, or village commune made up of peasant elders, was abolished and replaced by the kolkhoz administration headed by a chairman who was a party member usually from the towns. Party control was extended by employing teenagers as lookouts. Members of the Communist Young Pioneers organisation used wooden watchtowers to spy on the peasants in the fields to ensure they did not steal food to feed their own families.

The total cost in terms of human lives is difficult to quantify exactly. In 1929 Stalin had talked of the need to pass 'from limiting the exploitative tendencies of the kulaks to a policy of liquidating the kulaks as a class'. This class had been estimated to be about fifteen million in number. Historians' estimates of the number of deaths range from five to ten million. It was hardly surprising that some peasants cheered the invading German forces in 1941.

Although the political aim of ridding Soviet society of the kulaks was achieved, the economic results of collectivisation were more mixed. The slaughtering of animals by the kulaks had a serious effect on livestock numbers. Between 1928 and 1933 the number of cattle halved and this loss was not fully recovered until 1953. The consequence of this collapse was a shortage of meat and milk. Grain production also fell, declining from 73.3 million tonnes in 1928 to 67.6 million in 1934. This fall need not have been disastrous, but its impact on the countryside was pronounced due to the rise in grain seized by the government under the system of state procurements. The aim of producing enough food to feed the towns and the Red Army was achieved but only by taking much-needed supplies from the countryside. The rural population also starved in order to release food for export to gain much-needed foreign exchange. The result was a widespread famine in the years of 1932–33 which particularly affected the Ukraine, Kazakhstan and the Caucasus region. As peasants started to move into the towns in search of food the government introduced the passport system and peasants found it impossible to get a passport. They became effectively tied to the collective in a system which began to partly resemble that of **serfdom**, from which the peasants had supposedly been liberated in 1861. Unable to move from the collective, some peasants resorted to eating their own children in order to survive. The government officially denied any existence of famine, a claim supported by foreign visitors to the USSR, such as the British socialists Sidney and Beatrice Webb – but they had been escorted to model collectives well away from the famine areas. Recent research carried out on newly available Soviet data puts the number of famine-related deaths at four million for 1933 alone.

	1930	1931	1932	1933
Sheep and goats (millions)	108.8	77.7	52.1	50.2
Grain harvest (million tons)	83.5	69.5	69.6	68.4
Cattle (millions)	52.5	47.9	40.7	38.4
State procurements (million tons)	22.1	22.8	18.5	22.6
Pigs (millions)	13.6	14.4	11.6	12.1

Agricultural production during collectivisation (taken from Soviet sources)

A victim of the famine of 1932–33.

Summary of the results of collectivisation

Political:

- farming based on collective methods – e.g. the kolkhoz (collective farm) or the sovkhoz (state farm)
- heavy resistance from the peasantry to the process of collectivisation: property and animals destroyed by the peasants in order to prevent them falling into the hands of the government
- spread of party control to the countryside
- extended central government control over rural areas

Social:

- removal of the influence of traditional social roles – e.g. the village priest and school teacher
- removal of capitalist classes – e.g. elimination of kulaks (fifteen million people)
- abolition of peasant-controlled mir (village commune)

Economic:

- disastrous decline in number of cattle – halved between 1928 and 1933
- shortage of meat and milk
- fall in grain production from 73.3 million tonnes (1928) to 67.6 million tonnes (1934)
- widespread famine in rural areas leading to about four million deaths in 1933
- inadequate and chaotic planning and implementation of collectives
- greater use of machinery in countryside after mid-1930s
- grain supplies seized from peasants to feed towns and support growth in industrialisation: grain exports used to buy foreign exchange to help industry

The economic failure of collectivisation was partly due to inadequate planning and chaotic implementation of the policy. It was undertaken without the information needed to ensure success. The collectives were often too large and suffered from too much **central control** with party officials in Moscow giving orders to collectives which took little account of conditions on the ground. The mass movement of peasants from the countryside to the towns, which took place before the introduction of passports in 1933, had deprived the collectives of young able-bodied peasants and this proved a limitation to the success of the collectives. Another aspect of poor planning centred on the aim of mechanising agriculture. The push to collectivise was not coordinated with the manufacture of tractors or other agricultural machinery. It was not until the mid-1930s that the use of machinery became widespread on the collectives. The creation of **Motor Tractor Stations (MTS)** soon became despised by the peasants as agents of central control. The MTS not only provided machinery for the peasants but also political lectures on the benefits of socialism.

The divide between the town and the countryside was greatly deepened by collectivisation and the hostility it generated. The rather loose alliance between the peasants and the industrial workers, which had been created by the Bolsheviks during the revolution of 1917, was shattered with the imposition of a policy designed to sacrifice the needs of the countryside for those of the town.

KEY TERMS

Central control A term used to describe political control in the hands of the central government based in Moscow rather than leaving decisions in the hands of local people. This was a particular issue with the Russian peasants who resented interference by outsiders.

Motor Tractor Stations (MTS) Government-run centres which supplied farm machinery, such as tractors, to the collectives. They also provided advice on farming techniques and political lectures to persuade the peasants of the benefits of socialism and collectivisation. These centres rarely had enough machinery to meet demand and peasants viewed them as instruments of government interference in the countryside.

SUMMARY QUESTIONS

1 What were the economic reasons for collectivisation?

2 Who were the kulaks and why did Stalin want to eliminate them as a class?

3 Why was there so much opposition to collectivisation and how did Stalin deal with this?

4 Was collectivisation an economic success in the 1930s?

CHAPTER 4

The purges

KEY TERMS

The Great Purges The term used to describe the wave of terror which Stalin and his supporters used to remove enemies. The targets were so-called enemies of the state or people who were accused of crimes they often could not possibly have committed. Victims of the purges were either sent to labour camps or shot.

Show trials Public trials of leading enemies of the state. The proceedings were often filmed so that they could be used as propaganda in the cinemas. In this way they could be used to justify the actions taken against leading party members as well as being a warning to others.

Enemy of the people This term was used to describe those who were victims of the purges. Although it was a typical communist phrase, it was a vague term that enabled the government to take action on a range of supposed offences.

The use of **terror**, which had played a role in the communist hold on power since 1917, became a central part of the Soviet regime during the 1930s with the launching of the **Great Purges** against prominent party members. A series of **show trials** were held which saw former leaders of the regime accused and then, in nearly all cases, executed. Yet the purges were to extend beyond those former leaders who had fallen out with Stalin, to include army personnel and middle-ranking officials of the party. Anyone who could be labelled an '**enemy of the people**' might find themselves bundled away in the night by the secret police and never seen again.

By the early 1930s there was an extensive state machinery of terror. There was the Party Secretariat that collected information on Soviet citizens and party officials and also the secret police, known as the OGPU until 1934 and the NKVD thereafter, who were involved in surveillance of individuals and the running of labour camps. Thus, the apparatus was in place for dealing with opposition as and when it arose.

The event which triggered the Great Purges was the murder of **Kirov** in 1934. Opposition to Stalin's policies had started to grow with the launch of the first Five-Year Plan and collectivisation in 1928. Although the leaders of the Right of the party had been demoted or dismissed in 1929, their view that confrontation with the peasantry should be avoided came to the surface again in 1932 when collectivisation was leading to so much unrest in the countryside. The call for a more conciliatory approach was put forward in the Politburo, possibly by Kirov, and this posed a threat to Stalin's economic policies. Stalin may well have mistrusted Kirov because of his popularity in the party and because, as the party leader in Leningrad, Kirov's power base was the former centre of opposition that had supported Zinoviev. For these reasons it has been suggested that the murder of Kirov was carried out on Stalin's orders; certainly the NKVD did all they could to help the assassin kill Kirov. The official explanation was that Kirov's assassin was a member of an opposition group led by Zinoviev and Kamenev and, in a pattern which was to become familiar, one arrest led to the implication and arrest of others usually on trumped-up charges. Both Zinoviev and Kamenev were arrested, brought to trial and sentenced to long terms of imprisonment. Thus the murder of Kirov was the event which prompted the purging of large sections of the Communist Party.

The purge of the Left

During 1935 and 1936 there was a wave of denunciations and arrests of members of the **Left Opposition** who were still at large. Party members were advised to be vigilant against the 'enemies of the people' in all their disguises. This led to a series of show trials of leaders of the Left including Zinoviev and Kamenev in August 1936. They

Sergei Kirov.

KEY TERMS

The Left Opposition Those in the party who had supported the call for 'Permanent Revolution' in the 1920s. This put them against Stalin who had called for 'Socialism in One Country'. The Left had also called for rapid industrialisation and the abandonment of the NEP before Stalin was ready to do so. Because the Left were associated with the views of Trotsky it was relatively easy to attack them as enemies of the state. Trotsky, although he had fled abroad, continued to denounce Stalin. Zinoviev and Kamenev were the two most prominent members of the Left; both were accused of being Trotsky's agents.

The Right Opposition Those party members who had wished to keep the NEP and criticised Stalin's rapid industrialisation under the Five-Year Plans as harsh and, in economic terms, unnecessary. The leading member of the Right was Bukharin whose criticisms of Stalin's economic policies sealed his fate. He was executed in 1938.

Instruments of Stalin's terror

- The Party Secretariat collected information on party members which could be used to condemn them as enemies of the people.
- The Secret Police (NKVD) carried out surveillance, arrests and executions. They also ran the labour camps where many victims of the purges were imprisoned.

---

were accused of working as Trotsky's agents to undermine the state. Under severe pressure from the NKVD they confessed to crimes they could not possibly have carried out, including the murder of Kirov. They also implicated others in the conspiracy including the former leaders of the Right: Tomsky, Bukharin and Rykov.

The purge of party officials

In 1937 the purges saw a change in emphasis as show trials dealt with accusations of wrecking and sabotage in industry. Party officials such as Radek and Pyatakov were accused of working for Trotsky and foreign governments to undermine the Soviet economy. Their real crime was probably criticising the Five-Year Plans. Pyatakov had referred to mistakes made in economic policy.

The purge of the Right

By 1938 the machinery of terror was ready to strike against former leaders of the **Right Opposition**. Tomsky had committed suicide before he could be brought to trial but Bukharin and Rykov were accused of forming a 'Trotskyite-Rightist Bloc', a crime to which they both confessed. There was no hard evidence of these links with Trotsky but it was true that the Right had expressed opposition to the Five-Year Plans. Bukharin's article 'Notes of an Economist' made clear some of his criticisms of Stalin's economic policies. As a threat to Stalin he had to go.

The purge of the Red Army

It was not only the party leadership that suffered during the Great Terror; in 1937 and 1938 the Red Army also saw an extensive purge of personnel. Three out of the five marshals were purged, fourteen out of sixteen army commanders and 37,000 officers were either shot or imprisoned. The navy lost every one of its admirals during the purge. The usual accusation levelled against members of the armed forces was of links with foreign countries. There may well be some truth in this as a few army leaders did have contacts with the German army dating back to secret agreements, such as the Rapallo Treaty, signed between the two governments in the 1920s.

More likely than involvement in foreign conspiracies was the threat posed by the army's criticism of collectivisation. The peasantry, which provided a large percentage of rank and file soldiers, was demoralised by the hardships resulting from collectivisation and this was having a detrimental effect on army morale. For Stalin, the danger of these criticisms was made worse by the growth in the army's importance with the increase in defence resources in the 1930s. The power of the army leaders had to be cut down and this thorough purge would achieve this.

The purge of the secret police

With the purges, the amount of work generated for the secret police also grew and with it so did their influence. To ensure that the secret police posed no threat to Stalin, the purgers were themselves purged. In 1938 **Yagoda**, the former head of the NKVD, was shot. His replacement **Yezhov**, known as the 'bloody dwarf', oversaw the most excessive phase of the purges from 1936 to 1938. In the first six months as head of the secret police Yezhov purged over 3000 of its own personnel. The '**Yezhovschina**' came to an end when Yezhov was himself dismissed in 1938; his arrest in early 1939 was partly due to Stalin's need for a scapegoat for the excesses of the purges which were coming to an end.

Although the higher levels of the party suffered the most, there were sweeping purges at local level too. Denunciations of communist officials were partly driven by

Genrikh Yagoda (1891–1938) A member of the secret police since 1920, Yagoda advanced through the secret police until he was appointed Head of the NKVD in 1934. He implemented the early purges until he was himself purged in 1936. Stalin demoted Yagoda to a minor government position before having him shot in 1938.

Nicolai Yezhov (1895–1939) Replaced Yagoda as Head of the NKVD in 1936. Yezhov was particularly bloodthirsty, earning the nickname 'bloody dwarf'. His time as head of the NKVD was the most violent stage in the purges. He spent the first six months in office killing 3000 members of the secret police who had served under Yagoda. Yezhov was dismissed in 1938 before being executed in 1939. Stalin seems to have used him as a scapegoat for the excesses of the purges.

Yezhovschina The most violent stage of the purges from 1936 to 1938. Named after Yezhov, the head of the NKVD at the time.

Nicolai Yezhov, the 'bloody dwarf'.

a sense of justice. The old enemies: the kulaks, 'bourgeois experts' and Nepmen were rooted out as class enemies. Children were encouraged to inform on their parents if they suspected them of 'capitalist tendencies', and many did. Having contact with an accused person was dangerous, as was not doing your duty by informing on people you suspected. Hence the Soviet joke about two Russians talking in a park:

> FIRST MAN: What do you think of our great leader Stalin?
> SECOND MAN: Exactly the same as you, comrade.
> FIRST MAN: In that case I must arrest you.

Malice was responsible for some of the accusations, especially those against collective administrators. What also drove people to accuse others was the realisation that job opportunities were opened up by the removal of

Summary of the victims of the purges

The Left Opposition
Including:
- Zinoviev (1936)
- Kamenev (1936)
- Trotsky (1940)

The Right Opposition
Including:
- Tomsky (1936)
- Bukharin (1938)
- Rykov (1938)

Party officials
Including:
- all party leaders in the Soviet republics
- Radek and Pyatakov (1937)

Class enemies
Including:
- 15 million kulaks
- 'wreckers, saboteurs, spies'
- Nepmen
- bourgeois experts

The Red Army
Including:
- 3 out of 5 marshals
- 14 out of 16 army commanders
- 37,000 officers

The Secret Police
Including:
- over 3000 members of the secret police
- Yagoda (1938)
- Yezhov (1939)

KEY TERM

Gulag The term given to labour camps in the Soviet Union. It is an abbreviation for Main Prison Camp Administration. The camps were run by the secret police. There were over 100 Gulags and their inmates provided a useful source of slave labour for constructing roads and canals. The work of Gulag prisoners in the timber and mining industries made an important contribution to the economy.

'unworthy' comrades. The purges developed a dynamic of their own.

It is only since the collapse of the Soviet Union in 1991 and the subsequent opening up of archives that the true scale of the purges can be assessed. NKVD archives reveal a rise in **Gulag**, or labour camp, inmates of half a million between 1937 and 1939. Two-thirds of the 1.3 million inmates in 1939 were labelled as either 'political criminals' or 'socially harmful'. In addition to this, nearly three-quarters of a million people were executed rather than imprisoned.

Stalin's enemies saw the purges as evidence of his paranoid tendencies. Stalin seems to have mistrusted everyone, including members of his own family. To Trotsky, the purges were evidence of Stalin's betrayal of the revolution and his creation of a personal dictatorship. The sheer scale of the purges does, however, point to a degree of support for Stalin's actions and purges at local level, often driven by the pressure of rank and file communists to rid the USSR of its class enemies in all their disguises. In the atmosphere of terror, which existed in the 1930s, no one seemed safe. The fear of family members being taken away in the middle of the night was real for many citizens and had a lasting impact on life in the Soviet Union.

SUMMARY QUESTIONS

1 Why did the assassination of Kirov in 1934 lead to the start of the purges?

2 Who were the victims of the purges?

3 What was the 'Yezhovschina' and how did it come to an end?

4 What were the results of the purges for (a) the Red Army and (b) Stalin?

CHAPTER 5

Soviet society 1928–41

The years 1928–41 saw an enormous change in the Soviet economy, with the launch of the Five-Year Plan and collectivisation, and this in turn had a substantial impact on society. After 1928 the Soviet government launched what became known as a **'Cultural Revolution'**. The aim of this movement was to eliminate anyone considered to be a class enemy of socialism. This included technical experts, the Nepmen, kulaks and any person who exhibited signs of 'bourgeois values'. By attacking these social groups the government had clearly marked out a change from the more conciliatory policies of the NEP. The goal was now one of ensuring the dominance of the proletariat over society. Coupled with this was an attempt to mould a **'New Soviet Man'** by using instruments of social control, such as youth organisations and education, to change attitudes.

'Class enemies' – kulaks and Nepmen

The results of the so-called 'Cultural Revolution' would seem to have brought about a real change in Soviet society by ridding it of 'class enemies'. The policy of collectivisation, started in 1928, had a devastating impact on the kulaks. A class of over fifteen million was eliminated: by famine, by deportation to work camps and by genocide. This capitalist class of richer peasants who sold produce for profit was eradicated. The Shakhty show trial of 1928 signalled the government's intention to remove technical experts from industry. A group of engineers from the Shakhty region, accused of economic sabotage, were used as scapegoats for slow progress towards economic targets. This demonstrated that these technical experts were not to be allowed to stand in the way of the progress towards a socialist state. The first Five-Year Plan saw an increase in the number of attacks against 'bourgeois experts'. The private traders and 'Nepmen' who were seen as people who had gained under the compromises of the NEP at the expense of the proletariat were now swept aside as the Five-Year Plans brought nearly all sectors of the economy under state

KEY CONCEPTS

'Cultural Revolution' The name given to a movement aimed at eliminating capitalist, bourgeois elements from Soviet life and replacing them with Socialist values.

'New Soviet Man' A Soviet citizen who was fully moulded into the values of a committed Socialist.

control. The intelligentsia was also considered untrustworthy and bourgeois; they also found themselves under increasing restrictions and attack. Thus, in the removal of 'bourgeois class enemies' the policies launched in 1928 signified a substantial change in Soviet society.

The party structure

The purges of the 1930s went one stage further. They removed large numbers of people from within the party structure to open up job opportunities from within. This created a degree of social mobility, which had a fundamental impact on the way in which Soviet society developed thereafter. The removal of party officials considered 'suspect' opened the door for the promotion of party members of true proletarian origin. Workers were promoted into those management jobs in industry vacated by the removal of the 'bourgeois experts'. Over one and a half million workers gained management posts under the first Five-Year Plan. The expansion of higher education helped members of the industrial workforce gain the technical knowledge needed to achieve success in these appointments. Old party officials without technical expertise saw their position weaken. As Stalin stated in 1931: 'It's time the Bolsheviks themselves became experts'. Among those who, from a proletarian or peasant background, rose within the party structure during the thirties were **Khrushchev**, Kosygin and Brezhnev. This group came to dominate the party elite. They made up 50 per cent of the ministers and deputy ministers in 1953 when Stalin died and they were to dominate the Politburo until 1980. The new party elite had risen through a career ladder which became an important aspect of social mobility. The higher up this ladder you were the more privileges you received and these ranged from better housing, health care, access to special shops, chauffeured limousines and a 'dacha' (a villa for holidays) in the countryside. Promotion within this system was at the invitation of your superiors through a list of appointments known as the '**nomenklatura** system'. Remaining on the list from which appointments could be made required loyalty to your superiors. In the 1930s this was a tricky business as the purges resulted in a lot of job insecurity, yet the party was creating a new hierarchy which, with its desire to protect its own privileges, became increasingly conservative.

The trend towards appointing trained party members to positions of responsibility could also be seen in other areas of employment. The army, health care, education and the arts all saw a process of replacing 'experts' with loyal party members who had some training in the relevant field, a process which became partly supervised by government controlled trade unions. Those professionals who had been kept on after the revolution on account of their expertise could no longer be tolerated in an atmosphere of suspicion prompted by fear of the enemy within.

The peasantry

Party membership was the key to success in the Soviet Union of the 1930s but for the bulk of the population social conditions did not always change for the better. The peasantry fared much worse than the urban population due to the privations of collectivisation. Prices for agricultural products, which were fixed by the government, were kept low while state procurement payments were high. The rural population was squeezed for the benefit of the towns. That **social security** was not available in the countryside seemed to confirm the peasants as second-class citizens. The drift of population into the towns was hardly surprising.

The industrial workers

Conditions for the industrial workforce in towns were little better than those in the countryside. With the urban population rising from 29 million in 1929 to 40 million in 1933, the failure to address the needs of housing led to serious overcrowding and poor sanitation. Consumer goods were in short supply and food rationing had to be introduced to ensure adequate food supplies for industrial workers. The increase in industry under the Five-Year Plans resulted in the virtual disappearance of unemployment in the towns, but working conditions were harsh. The punctuality and discipline required for factory work caused particular problems for peasants moving to the towns for work. The Stakhanovite movement was an attempt to promote a more vigorous work ethic. Workers were encouraged to work like the hero Stakhanov but few were able to match his productivity and those model workers who did were often ridiculed by the rest of the workforce. Living conditions for the industrial workforce declined during the first Five-Year Plan and the trade unions, brought under strict government control, were in a weak position to press for improvements. The division between the government and the working class was widened still further.

The role of women and the family

After the revolution of 1917 women had been granted greater rights in marriage and measures had been introduced to make both divorce and abortion easier. Although these rights had later been restricted, women still had more rights than before the revolution. The Communist Party had set up a women's branch of the Central Committee, **Zhenotdel**, to promote the position of women within socialist notions of equality. The 1930s were to see important changes in women's roles.

KEY TERM

Zhenotdel The women's branch of the Central Committee of the Communist Party. It was closed down in 1930 when the party claimed that all women's issues had been solved.

In 1930 the party closed down Zhenotdel, claiming that women's issues had been solved. This was a reflection of the attitudes of the male-dominated party, which had always been half-hearted in its support for women's issues. Women remained grossly under-represented in the party. In fact, the policies of industrialisation and collectivisation were to have far-reaching consequences for women. Many women in the countryside found themselves deserted by husbands who left for jobs in the towns. Collectivisation came to rely more and more on the labour of women. In the towns women were given little choice but to work out of economic necessity. The number of female workers rose substantially in the 1930s, from three million in 1928 to over thirteen million in 1940. Given the labour shortages of the period the government was keen to encourage women to work although it was economic necessity more than government encouragement that drove women into work. More positively, the expansion in higher education provided new opportunities for women. In 1929 the government reserved 20 per cent of higher education places for women. This was a rather modest increase on the 14 per cent already occupied by women but, by 1940, over 40 per cent of engineering students were female. Women also gained a high percentage of jobs in the expanding areas of health care and education, although neither sector offered high wages. The position of women in the Muslim areas of the Soviet Union remained resistant to change for religious reasons.

Government changes in family policy gave women more freedom. To many communists the notion of family was an outmoded, capitalist tool. The Cultural Revolution involved pressures which aimed to destroy the traditional concept of the family. Divorce could be obtained on request and abortion was easily available. In Moscow, abortions outnumbered live births by three to one and the birth rate remained low. Yet these changes did not always improve the position of women. Women often found themselves deserted by men with no means of economic support. The break up of many families led to an increase in orphans who roamed the streets of many towns, to the concern of the authorities. The government decided to revert to more conservative policies.

By 1934 the government had become so concerned about the detrimental effects of family breakdowns that measures were introduced to raise the status of marriage and make divorce more expensive. 'Free' marriages – that is, those not formally registered with the state – lost their legal status and family responsibilities were to be taken seriously. As an attempt to raise the status of the family, the government introduced awards for 'mother-heroines' who had ten or more children. Male homosexuality was declared illegal in 1936 and abortion was outlawed during this **'Great Retreat'** in family policy. The idea of the family as an unnecessary 'bourgeois' concept was replaced by the view that the family was a necessary unit of socialist society. Traditional values were reasserted.

Komsomol

The young may have suffered considerably through changes to the family but they were at the forefront of the Cultural Revolution. The ideals of the movement provided them with some purpose and the communist youth organisation, **Komsomol**, took an important role in rooting out class

ОВЛАДЕВАЯ ТЕХНИКОЙ, БУДЬ В ПЕРВЫХ
РЯДАХ СТРОИТЕЛЕЙ СОЦИАЛИЗМА

Soviet poster of women at work.

enemies. After the compromises of the NEP the Cultural
Revolution was seen as a more radical step towards the
socialist utopia that many radical young communists
aspired to. The removal of the 'old guard' opened up a
whole range of job opportunities for young, eager
communists. One area, which was greatly influenced by the
campaigning of Komsomol, was that of education. Their
attacks on 'bourgeois' elements in education removed many
teachers and led to the collapse of education departments in
many parts of the country. The government was forced to

intervene in order to restore order. The Education Law of 1935 put greater emphasis on discipline in schools and the curriculum was placed under stricter government control.

Education

The Cultural Revolution had resulted in widespread disruption to the education system, which caused the government concern, as the importance of education in shaping society was recognised by the government. From 1935 onwards there was a series of measures designed to impose control over education. Textbooks were prescribed by the government and formal examinations were reintroduced. By the end of the 1930s the system had returned to a more traditional basis, including compulsory pigtails for girls. One new element introduced was the teaching of communist ideology as a compulsory subject. Higher education saw the same trend. The quota system of entry to higher education, which had been introduced in 1929, was abolished in 1935. The quota system allowed entry to higher education based on social class, with 70 per cent of places reserved for those of working class origin. This figure was reached only once and attempts to meet it led to a drop-out rate of 70 per cent as many students failed to finish courses they were ill-prepared for. The end of the quota system put the emphasis in higher education back on quality rather than quantity and, as the percentage of working class students fell, the **intelligentsia** gained. Despite the return to a more traditional approach in education after 1935, there were some lasting changes. Opportunities for students from working class backgrounds remained better than the situation before 1928. The education system was now more focused on technical and scientific learning in order to meet the needs of the Five-Year Plans. While education was targeted mainly at the young, a literacy campaign was launched to ensure that their parents had the basic skills needed to contribute to the economy.

The church

Komsomol attacks on bourgeois elements were also directed at the church. Although severely restricted after the 1917 revolution, the Church still presented a danger as an instrument of an alternative ideology. Komsomol

KEY TERM

Intelligentsia Intellectuals who wanted to use education as a method of promoting free thinking.

Red Army soldiers looting Church property.

groups carried out attacks on the remnants of the Church during the collectivisation process and many priests were hounded out of villages. The government introduced a further series of repressive measures in 1929, which included the requirement of congregations and their places of worship to be registered with the government. The organisation of the Russian Orthodox Church still existed, but a wave of arrests between 1936 and 1939 severely reduced the number of bishops. Yet there is also evidence of an increase in the number of people worshipping in secret during the insecurity of the purges.

CONCLUSION

Between 1928 and 1941 Soviet society underwent an enormous change. The removal of large numbers of class enemies had provided opportunities for a new structure to take shape. A hierarchy based on the party and its privileges was emerging and, although there was greater social mobility for those from working class and peasant backgrounds, it was the dominance of the party, not the proletariat, which had been achieved. This development was reinforced by the reimposition of more traditional and conservative values by the government after the excesses of the Cultural Revolution. In this sense the change, which had occurred, was both controlled and restricted.

SUMMARY QUESTIONS

1 How did the position of the following change during the period 1928–41?
   a) the peasantry
   b) industrial workers
   c) women.

2 How did the Cultural Revolution affect the education system during the early 1930s?

3 How was the influence of the Church reduced during the 1930s?

CHAPTER 6

Popular culture and the arts

Popular culture This refers to those art forms which are geared towards the general population and a mass audience. Popular fiction, the radio and cinema are usually placed in this category.

Bourgeois culture A term used by the communists to refer to art forms, such as traditional ballet, opera and fine art, which were geared to an exclusive and elitist audience. They were seen as products of the bourgeoisie.

Although the government had become aware of the value of using the arts and **popular culture** for their own purposes by 1924, they had not enforced rigid control over this sphere of activity. After 1924 there was a much more concerted attempt by the government to use culture for their own ends. The **Cultural Revolution** of 1928–32 saw the arts and popular culture become a key battleground as the party tried to root out all elements of **bourgeois culture** and construct a new Soviet culture which reinforced socialist values and the policies of the government. By the mid-1930s the government was concerned that the Cultural Revolution was getting out of hand and the party leadership took measures to bring cultural policy under its control. Although socialist values were promoted through **Socialist Realism** (see page 57), accommodation had to be made with the needs of the leadership. The development of a cult of personality around Stalin was evidence that, instead of serving the needs of socialism, culture became more of an instrument of the party leadership.

The aims of Soviet cultural policy

- to remove all traces of 'bourgeois' culture
- to use culture as a means of instilling socialist values in the Soviet people
- to present the population with positive images of the achievements of socialism and life in the Soviet Union
- to support government policy

By the end of the 1930s two additional aims were in evidence:

- to promote a cult of personality around Stalin
- to encourage patriotism and Russian nationalism in the face of the growing threat of war

---

The Cultural Revolution

The greater freedom in the arts which had been tolerated under Lenin came under growing criticism in the late 1920s. Caught up in the pressures which led to the Five-Year Plan and collectivisation, the Cultural Revolution became part of the attempt to sweep away the old 'bourgeois' elements within society. This entailed a full-scale assault on the intelligentsia and cultural elites. Those **Fellow Travellers** tolerated under Lenin were to be removed and replaced by artists whose loyalty to socialism was not in question. The ideas of the **Constructivists** gained the upper hand.

Making use of young communists, Komsomol enthusiasts were encouraged to root out and attack 'bourgeois' elements. Theatre productions of suspect plays were disrupted by booing and whistling. In literature the **Russian Association of Proletarian Writers (RAPP)** made increasingly bitter attacks on the Fellow Travellers and condemned the decadent **individualism** of writers who adopted new experimental techniques. RAPP preferred works which stressed the achievements of the workers in what became termed the **cult of the 'little man'**. Kataev's novel *Time Forward* (1932) was a good example of this. It recounted the story of a record-breaking shift at Magnitogorsk steel works. This sort of theme, described by Sheila Fitzpatrick as 'Boy meets Girl meets Tractor', tied in with the Five-Year Plans but it soon lost its popularity as similar themes were endlessly repeated. Yet RAPP did its best to encourage cultural activities in factories with some success.

The Cultural Revolution not only aimed to destroy elements of 'bourgeois' culture; it also encouraged visions of what the new socialist culture should be like. This led to a brief flowering of **visionary utopianism** which had little to do with practical politics. Building on **Futurism**, these visionaries took the opportunity to put forward ideas for a socialist future. Plans were drawn up for new cities involving communal living in large apartments. Architecture was seen by some as an instrument which could be used to destroy traditional family life. These ideas were too radical for many party members and by the end of the first Five-Year Plan the government was ready to

KEY TERMS

Cultural Revolution The movement by Communist Party activists to purge all aspects of the culture of 'bourgeois' elements.

'Fellow Travellers' A term applied to those artists who, while not being communists, were sympathetic to the ideas of Communism.

Constructivists Those who wished to create a new proletarian culture based on the worker and industrial technology.

The Russian Association of Proletarian Writers (RAPP) This was an organisation that controlled the publication of books to ensure that they promoted the values of socialism.

Individualism A term used to stress the importance of free thought and action by individuals in the pursuit of art. The communists disliked this emphasis, preferring artists to follow the guidelines laid down by the government.

Cult of the 'little man' The writing of novels that glorified the achievements of the industrial worker and collective peasant. It was encouraged by the government and was a criticism of 'bourgeois' writing, which often focused on wealthy people of high status.

restore control over cultural organisations. The Cultural Revolution had removed most of the old intelligentsia and replaced it with Soviet intellectuals. With more communist personnel in place, the time was now considered ripe for a change in emphasis as the government focused more on the content of Soviet culture.

Socialist Realism

In 1932 the party leadership announced that RAPP would be closed down and replaced by a new Union of Soviet

Socialist Realism: an idealised representation of Molotov and Stalin with their children.

Writers. This was, in effect, bringing the Cultural Revolution to an end. Stalin recognised the importance of writers, calling them 'engineers of human souls', and all writers were to be co-ordinated by the new body in the pursuit of Socialist Realism. This term was deliberately vague so as to avoid being too narrow, but included works which were 'rooted in the people' and conveyed a sense of reality. Many classic writers of the past such as Tolstoy, Charles Dickens and Emile Zola were considered to be relevant to the origins of Socialist Realism. Thus the works of others were used for the purpose of the regime. There was a change of emphasis away from the cult of the 'little man' to heroes connected with the party. The standard plot of literature in the 1930s was of a hero from the people who is guided by the party to greater things. This theme was developed in much of the 'high' literature through works by Sholokhov and Gorki and had much in common with traditional Russian folk stories. 'Lowbrow' literature was usually concerned with heroes from Russian history, war stories or detective novels where a police agent thwarts the evil capitalists. The low price of these books and the tenfold growth in library acquisitions ensured the population had easy access to this material. Through government agencies the party controlled what was published and by whom. Some writers, such as **Zoshchenko**, conformed to the rules but the quality of their work suffered, others refused to work under such restrictions and emigrated. **Pasternak** and **Anna Akhamatova** gave up writing, opting for what Babel called 'the genre of silence'. Mayakovsky, who had become disillusioned with the party, committed suicide; others met their deaths in the labour camps.

Increased government interference was also evident in the Soviet press. Newspapers such as *Pravda* and *Izvestiya* carried less real information and the range of views expressed narrowed. They were more likely to cover economic achievements with statistics quoted to highlight areas of success alongside demands to work even harder. Western-style adverts for the latest film were no longer carried. The press became a propaganda sheet for the government.

Boris Pasternak (1890–1960) One of the leading literary figures in Soviet history. Pasternak wrote poetry in the 1920s and early 1930s but he was criticised by the Soviet authorities for failing to follow the guidelines of Socialist Realism. He gave up writing for publication and translated the works of Shakespeare and other English writers into Russian. His most famous work, the novel *Dr Zhivago*, was rejected by the Soviet authorities but was smuggled abroad for publication in 1957.

Mikhail Zoshchenko (1895–1958) Soviet writer who produced satires on everyday life. His acid comments did not please the government. Under pressure from the authorities, he produced work which promoted Social Realism but it was of poor quality compared to his earlier works.

Dmitri Shostakovich (1906–1975) Composer of classical music. His works were well received by the public but criticised by the party for counter-revolutionary tendencies. His opera *Lady Macbeth of Mtensk* (1935) was condemned by Stalin. He wrote symphonies, musical scores, opera and ballet music. Although constantly censored by the government, he was able to maintain a high standard of work.

KEY TERMS

'Pravda' The main daily newspaper of the USSR. *Pravda* (truth) was the official newspaper of the Communist Party.

'Izvestiya' A popular daily newspaper in the USSR. *Izvestiya* (news) was the official newspaper of the national government.

Stalinist baroque The term used to describe the style of architecture favoured by Stalin in the 1930s. It was a style that made use of classical lines and elaborate decoration on a grand scale and is sometimes referred to as 'wedding cake' architecture. Good examples included the Moscow University building and the Moscow metro stations. It was architecture designed to impress.

Music also suffered from a pressure to toe the line. In 1935 Stalin walked out of a performance of **Shostakovich's** opera *Lady Macbeth of Mtensk*, a politically correct story of adultery, due to 'discordant notes'. The real reason was Stalin's shock at the bedroom scene where trombones were used to underline what was happening. Like literature, it was better to stick to well-worn themes than experiment if you wished to carry on working.

The field of science was more immune to ideological interference but few scientists would present a theory until Stalin's approval had been received. This resulted in the promotion of the ideas of **Trofim Lysenko** on remedies for plant breeding which had little scientific basis but

Moscow University.

originated from the peasantry. Lysenko was hailed as the expert in 'proletarian science'.

In architecture the visionary ideas of the Cultural Revolution gave way to '**Stalinist baroque**', better known as 'wedding cake' architecture (see page 59). Many public buildings were built in this style which made use of classical lines, the best example being Moscow University which was rebuilt after 1945. The Moscow metro system was another fine example of Stalinist baroque with stations decorated using elaborate murals, showing the endeavours of the workers, and chandeliers. The centre of Moscow was said to have resembled a building site in the 1930s as processional ways were created so that soldiers could march on Red Square from six directions during parades.

Art was also harnessed by the regime to project ideal images of life under the Five-Year Plans. Socialist Realism led to a rejection of abstract art as posters, paintings and sculptures presented images of the worker and peasant, often together, working for socialism and gaining strength through their efforts (page 61). Vast statues of Stalin started to appear in addition to the numerous ones of Lenin. Paintings and photographs constantly had to be revised as people fell out of favour during the purges of the 1930s. Group photos were a particular problem for the official retouchers, as a group of fifteen would be gradually reduced to perhaps seven.

The achievements of the revolution were conveyed through films such as **Eisenstein**'s *October* (1927) which presented the heroic version of the storming of the Winter Palace in 1917. This served the interests of the government in presenting the revolution as a mass movement. Unfortunately, due to Eisenstein's excessive use of extras, more people died in the making of the film than in the actual events themselves.

The cult of personality

By the end of the 1930s it was clear that Socialist Realism was being used to reinforce the policies of the party as well as socialist values and that these two elements were not necessarily the same thing. The emergence of a **cult of**

Trofim Lysenko (1898–1976) An agricultural scientist, whose theories on genetics rejected established views. He was hailed by Stalin as a proletarian scientist but his theories were largely bogus, based on little scientific research. The application of Lysenko's theories to Soviet agriculture proved disastrous.

Sergei Eisenstein (1898–1948) Cinema film producer who was prepared to use his talents to support the Soviet government. His most important films included *Battleship Potemkin* (1925) and *October* (1927). Eisenstein's work was technically excellent and innovative. It showed that high quality art could still be produced under the Soviet regime. Eisenstein fell out of favour with the government in the mid-1930s for failing to follow Socialist Realism but decided to follow the government line. Restored to favour, he produced *Alexander Nevsky* in 1938, a film about a mediaeval Russian prince who repelled a German attack. The film fitted the mood of a Soviet people growing increasingly concerned about war.

Cult of personality The adoration of an individual through the use of art and popular culture.

A Soviet propaganda poster from the 1930s.

personality centred on Stalin was the most telling example of this. All forms of the arts and popular culture were used to highlight the personal qualities of Stalin and praise his every action. Stalin was presented as Lenin's closest colleague, a hero of the civil war and the saviour of the revolution in the face of assaults from its enemies such as Leftists and Rightists. Artists set to work presenting images of 'the big hero' or *Vozhd* (the boss). Portraits of Stalin turned the rough Georgian peasant into an image of a Hollywood film star, but it did require a lot of soft focus! Marfa Kriukova's *The Tale of Lenin* was a folk tale with Lenin represented by the sun and Trotsky as the dark villain. The tale concluded with the sun sending out light to defeat the dark villain. Stalin was, of course, the light. This cult of personality can be seen as part of what Trotsky called turning a 'dictatorship of the proletariat' into a personal dictatorship of Stalin.

The growing threat of world war

As the threat of future war grew in the late 1930s there was a change in emphasis in Soviet cultural policy. The party leadership recognised the need to get across values which would bind the Soviet people together in the event of an attack. In the arts and popular culture, this led to an emphasis on **nationalism** and patriotism. Eisenstein's film *Alexander Nevsky* (1938) reflected this trend. The German invasion of 1941 had an enormous impact on all aspects of Soviet life and required Soviet citizens to devote all their energies to the defence of the country. This could be achieved only by appealing to a deep sense of Russian patriotism. As Stalin declared in 1941: 'Let the images of our great ancestors inspire you during this war'. The result was an even greater emphasis than before the war on past military leaders and national heroes such as Kutuzov, the hero of the war against Napoleon.

One aspect of popular culture which did cause the government some concern was the radio. As in most countries at the start of the war the Soviet government took measures to ensure news of the front was censored. Soviet citizens had to hand in their private radio sets. This ensured that the only news received was from public loudspeakers issued by the government and not from the BBC or German news stations. Despite this restriction, artists were generally more free to express themselves than before the war, yet they hardly needed much encouragement to deal with topics which promoted nationalism and patriotism. These values were useful to the government after the start of the war but marked a move away from Socialist Realism under party control.

CONCLUSION

It would be misleading to present Soviet arts and popular culture in the period 1924–41 as remaining constant. Although the period was dominated by government interference and control for its own ends, the extent of the

Nationalism The feeling of pride in one's own nation and national identity. In terms of the USSR, nationalism was a complex issue as the country was made up of many different national groups. In practice Russian nationalism was the dominant force and was often imposed on minority groups.

Summary of themes presented through Soviet arts and popular culture

Machines and technology
- promoted by the Constructivists – e.g. Tatlin in the early 1920s
- related to using technology to build a new future
- glorified objects which represented the worker or peasant

Futurism
- emphasis on exploring the possibilities of the future
- attacked traditional assumptions of 'bourgeois' art
- influenced visionary utopianism – e.g. using architecture to create a new society based on communal living

Socialist Realism
- art which was 'rooted in the people' – e.g. workers/peasants
- idealistic representations of Soviet life in a realistic style
- emphasis on how the party could guide people to greater things

The cult of personality
- highlighted Stalin and attributed positive qualities to him
- presented Stalin as a superhero through statues and paintings
- pronounced from the mid-1930s onwards

Nationalism
- emphasis on Russian heroes – e.g. Nevsky, Kutuzov
- used stories from traditional folk tales
- linked to the need for patriotism during the Second World War
- became increasingly xenophobic during the Zhdanovshchina (a purge of cultural activity after 1945)

government's role and its aims did vary with the circumstances and the requirements of the party leadership. Despite the directives issued by the government there was some variety in the content produced and although restrictions were generally oppressive there were those prepared to push the boundaries of what was acceptable. Nonetheless, the overall picture is of a party leadership using the arts and popular culture as instruments of social control to maintain their political power.

SUMMARY QUESTIONS

1 What were the aims of the Cultural Revolution?

2 What was Socialist Realism and what impact did it have on the arts in the Soviet Union during the 1930s?

3 What evidence is there for the development of a cult of personality around Stalin in the 1930s?

4 Study the illustrations on pages 57 and 61.
   a) What messages are the artists trying to get across?
   b) How reliable are these sources as evidence of life in the Soviet Union during the 1930s?

AS ASSESSMENT: LIFE IN THE SOVIET UNION 1928–41

USING HISTORICAL SOURCES

Comprehension of sources

At AS Level you are likely to be asked questions that are designed to test your ability to comprehend historical sources as part of structured questions on the topic you are studying. When considering sources it is necessary to bear in mind four key questions:

i) **Who?** Who is the author of the source? Is it by a historian (and from which school of thought), a politician, a factory owner or a trade unionist? If you are presented with a poster or painting, the artist's name may be unfamiliar or it may not even be stated. The content may suggest that the artist was either supporting or criticising the regime and its achievements. The background of the artist/author may affect the style and content of the source. It is important to consider their values and attitudes as these may be reflected in the source.

ii) **What?** What does the source tell us? What is the content of the source? Does it ignore or neglect certain aspects? What a source does not say can also be important. It is always worth thinking about the overall thrust of a source. The rest of the content may well be the development of one basic point. It is also useful to consider the style, language and tone of the source as this often helps you to 'read between the lines' of what is stated. Cartoonists often make use of exaggeration and humour to make their point but there has to be some truth, or at least perceived truth, behind the exaggeration otherwise no one will get the joke let alone the message. Posters, too, aim to convey a message by simplification and sometimes exaggeration. As with cartoons, it is necessary to consider both the message and the techniques employed to convey it. Photographs can give a valuable snapshot of life at the time but you should always consider carefully whether the photograph presents a typical or untypical picture of the wider context. To assess this you will need to refer to your own knowledge; for example, a photo of peasants happily at work on a collective in 1932 would not be representative of the peasants' response to collectivisation in large parts of the Soviet Union.

iii) **When?** When was the source produced? Accounts produced at the time of the event have the advantage of immediacy; accounts written later have the advantage of hindsight. The fact that an author was an eyewitness could give a source considerable value.

iv) **Why?** Why was the source produced? What is the purpose of the source? Is it propaganda? What is the motive of the author? Why was there a need to convey the message? This can be related to a consideration of the intended audience. A poster showing the successes of the Five-Year Plans despite criticisms from capitalists may be aimed at both 'bourgeois' elements within the USSR and the international community who doubted their success.

A consideration of these questions will enable you to evaluate sources in detail with reference to their usefulness, reliability and value. Avoid stock answers such as 'all cartoons are exaggerated and therefore unreliable' or 'photographs show only one moment in time'. Remember that you are being asked to examine a specific source or sources and your evaluation must be based on this rather than comments about sources in general.

Remember also that source-based questions are designed to test your skills in **understanding and using sources** as a historian and this is what you need to show in your answer.

QUESTIONS REQUIRING EXTENDED ANSWERS

Deconstructing questions

As a student of history you are required to produce extended answers in the form of essays. At AS Level these will be structured essays, often broken down into two parts. These questions are designed to test your ability in understanding historical issues and using information to support your views in the form of an argument.

Essay writing is rather like producing a report in that it is important to organise material into a logical sequence. In order to ensure that this is done effectively it is important to be aware of the demands of the question. **You ignore the question at your peril!**

If you spend time thinking about the question and planning your answer you will save time later. This will also ensure that time is not wasted writing an inappropriate and irrelevant essay. A useful tool for planning is that of **deconstructing questions.**

One of the most common reasons for under-performing in exams is the failure to produce a relevant answer. By using the following process you will be able to plan your essays to ensure that the specific question asked is directly addressed.

How to deconstruct a question

Break the question down into its constituent parts. Look for the following:

1. The **instruction** (I) e.g. 'examine', 'what'.
2. The **topic** (T) e.g. Five-Year Plans, collectivisation.
3. **Keywords** (KW) which need to be focused upon in your answer.

Example:

What were the aims of Soviet policy towards women and the family between 1928 and 1941?

I – 'What'
T – Soviet policy towards women and the family
KW – 'aims', 'women and the family', '1928–41'.

Types of structured essay questions

Essay questions can be divided into various categories depending on the instruction given. It is useful to think about the demands of each type of question.

1 **Cause/effect questions** These questions usually start with 'why' or 'what'. For example, why did the Soviet Union embark on a policy of rapid industrialisation between 1928 and 1941? For this type of question a list of factors provides a useful starting point but there is the danger that each factor is described rather than assessed. Think about dividing the factors into those which were economic and those which were political. It is also essential to assess the relative importance of each factor. This will help you to develop an argument rather than just describe a list of factors involved.

2 **Discussion questions** These quite often appear as a statement followed by the word 'discuss' or the phrase 'Do you agree?'. For example, 'Despite the human cost the Five-Year Plans of the 1930s were an economic success.' 'Do you agree?' The best way of dealing with this sort of question is to consider the evidence both for and against the statement given.

3 **Significance/importance questions** These questions often start with phrases such as 'assess', 'how far' or 'to what extent'; instructions which require you to weigh up the significance/importance of a given factor. Example: Assess the impact of the Cultural Revolution on popular culture and the arts in the Soviet Union between 1928 and 1941. This question would require an examination of the significance of the Cultural Revolution as well as its limitations. If the Cultural Revolution was limited in its impact, the reasons for this would need to be discussed.

4 **Compare/contrast questions** These questions can be notoriously difficult for students. The key point to remember here is to ensure that the instruction is

obeyed. For example, if asked to compare and contrast the impact of the Five-Year Plans on industry with that their impact on agriculture it is quite common for students to describe industrial and agricultural developments separately with no real comparison until the conclusion. It is much better to think of headings under which they can be directly compared and contrasted, e.g. aims, economic impact – successes and failures, social impact, political impact, etc.

Planning essays

After deconstructing a question you are in a better position to draw up a relevant plan for the essay. It is worth spending time thinking about your overall argument and how it will be developed through the essay in a series of paragraphs/sections each looking at a different aspect. There is, of course, no model answer at this level but some general principles can be applied.

A general essay plan

1. Introduction. State your overall argument; do not leave this to the conclusion. Make it clear what you will be looking at in the essay to develop your argument.
2. Main content. Each section should develop your argument by looking at a particular area or aspect. For each paragraph:
   a) make the point(s)
   b) explain it in relation to the question
   c) support your point with precise evidence
3. Conclusion. This should sum up your argument and response to the question.

AN EXAMPLE OF A STRUCTURED QUESTION IN THE STYLE OF EDEXCEL

Source A

A painting commissioned by the government in the 1930s.

Question 1
a) Study Source A.
   What message, about rural life in the Soviet Union during the 1930s, is the artist of Source A trying to convey?
b) Why was there a lot of resistance to collectivisation in the Soviet Union between 1928 and 1935?
c) To what extent had the policy of collectivisation achieved its aims by 1941?

How you should answer these questions.
Question (a): This question is designed to assess your ability to comprehend a source. The source can be understood at a range of levels and this would be recognised in the mark scheme for this question.

Mark scheme
LEVEL 1: A simple statement which takes the source at face value.
LEVEL 2: A developed statement, supported by reference to the source and which makes some attempt to place the source within its wider context.
LEVEL 3: A full examination of the purpose of the author relating the content of the source to the wider context of agricultural developments in the 1930s and opposition to them.

Source A, at face value, presents a view of peasants happily working in the fields. But on deeper examination there is a range of messages the artist is trying to convey. The image presented by the artist is romanticised with the peasants wearing traditional clothes and carrying farming implements. The vegetation implies a fertile and productive land which can support large numbers of peasants. The people shown in the painting are all women and this stresses their role in Soviet farming. The women seem to be working in a group which implies collectivisation has taken place; certainly there is an emphasis on the group rather than the individual, and smiling faces indicate a countryside at peace with itself. This is clearly the image the Soviet government wished to put across and the painting is a typical example of Socialist Realism used in art by the government to present an idealised view of developments under Socialism. The reality was somewhat different as collectivisation resulted in widespread disruption of agriculture, violent opposition and famine. Peasants in the Ukraine would hardly recognise this picture of the countryside in the 1930s.

Question (b): This question is designed to assess your ability to recall, understand and use factual information. You will be marked according to **the level of understanding** you show in response to the question.

Mark scheme
LEVEL 1: Simple statement which identifies one reason.
LEVEL 2: A statement that identifies more than one reason with some development, although this may be focused on one reason with others treated briefly.
LEVEL 3: A developed statement with assessment of a range of reasons. At the top of this level will be answers with a secure and confident assessment of the relative importance of the different reasons and the links between them.

Answers to this question could identify a range of reasons: such as the hostility of the kulaks to losing privately owned land; the peasants' resentment of government interference; the lack of support for the urban-based Communist Party and Communism in the countryside; the heavy-handed methods used by Party officials in implementing collectivisation; the high level of state procurements of foodstuffs and the resulting famine; the role of nationalist feeling in areas such as the Ukraine against the Soviet state. The theme of imposing central political control could be developed as a way of showing links between these various factors.

Question (c): This question requires a mini-essay to show your ability to present a reasoned argument using the concept of consequence. A typical mark scheme would be as follows:

LEVEL 1: Information relevant to the question is presented but there is no explicit argument OR a viewpoint is presented but the evidence used is so brief that it is little more than an assertion.
LEVEL 2: A developed statement, supported by some examples, but the argument is not sustained. There may be a drift into description with a link to the specific focus of the question at the end.
LEVEL 3: A developed explanation with sustained relevance. Factual information may not be wide-ranging but it is focused on the question and used to develop an argument. There will be a consideration of both policy successes and failures to address 'to what extent'.
LEVEL 4: A sustained, coherent argument with thorough and precise detail used to develop points. Policy successes and failures will both be assessed in order to come to a reasoned judgement.

A2 SECTION: STALIN AND THE SOVIET UNION 1924–41

INTRODUCTION

> ### Key questions
> - Why did Stalin emerge as leader of the Soviet Union between 1924 and 1929?
> - How did Stalin exercise political control?
> - Did Stalin preserve or destroy Bolshevism?
> - How successful was Stalin's attempt to modernise the USSR?
> - How popular was Stalin?

Stalin is a controversial subject for historians: his policies saw the rapid industrialisation of the Soviet Union alongside unprecedented hardship and human slaughter. It is therefore not surprising that historians have engaged in a series of very active debates concerning Stalin and his policies.

The rise of Stalin to a position of supreme power has been traced back to a range of factors varying from the force of Stalin's own personality to the structures and circumstances found in the Soviet Union in the 1920s. Stalin's victory in the power struggle that followed Lenin's death in 1924 was mirrored in the defeat of his rivals, especially Trotsky and Bukharin, whose ideas might have offered the Russian Revolution an alternative course of events. By 1929 Stalin was in a position to impose his own policies which were to have an enormous impact on all aspects of life in the Soviet Union. These policies, which together established what has become known as Stalinism, have been hotly debated. Industrialisation and collectivisation can be seen as attempts to modernise a backward Soviet economy but they were also methods by which Stalin and the Communist Party could extend their own control over a vast country. The purpose of terror and propaganda, as they were used by the Soviet leadership, can be seen either as instruments to beat the population into submission or as methods to safeguard the Revolution. This has led to a consideration of the nature of the Stalinist state and of the importance of Stalin's role and influence within it. Did Stalinism represent the consolidation of socialism and ensure the survival of the Revolution or was it, as Trotsky argued, a betrayal of the Revolution for Stalin's own ends?

These historical issues are still influenced by present-day attitudes and are likely to be the source of continuing disagreement. History may be concerned with the past but our views of it are changing all the time. The dilemmas of the past are often echoed in those of the present.

SECTION 1

Why did Stalin emerge as leader of the Soviet Union between 1924 and 1929?

WHY DID STALIN, AND NOT TROTSKY, EMERGE AS LEADER OF THE SOVIET UNION BETWEEN 1924 AND 1929?

From the collective leadership which ruled the Soviet Union after Lenin's death, Stalin emerged as the dominant figure, removing his colleagues and establishing his position as sole leader of the state. To most other members of the Communist Party in 1924 this development would have been viewed as unlikely because the majority of the party saw Trotsky as the most likely successor to Lenin. Stalin was seen as an administrator and a rather dull personality. Yet it was not just a matter of personality. Stalin was undoubtedly skilful in using the circumstances that presented themselves in 1924 and the opportunities that arose thereafter to overcome his opponents in the party. Important changes had occurred within the party structure and within its membership and Stalin showed enormous political shrewdness and skill in not only being aware of these changes, but also positioning himself so that he could benefit from them and use the situation to his advantage. By 1929 Stalin had secured his position as sole leader of the Soviet Union and in doing so he had defeated Trotsky and neutralised his rivals in the Politburo.

The main factors leading to the rise of Stalin were:
1. Differences in personality
When comparing Stalin and Trotsky it is clear that they were very different personalities and this fact had a significant bearing on how they reacted to the circumstances that presented themselves after 1924.

Stalin's early life gives some indications of personality traits that were to come to the fore after 1924. His Georgian, peasant background made him an outsider in Russian revolutionary circles but he had learnt to be self-reliant. As a young man he was influenced by socialism and developed a deep sense of class hatred. Although his understanding of Marxist ideology was limited, Stalin was able to bring other qualities to the revolutionary movement. His bank robbing activities aimed at helping to fund the Bolshevik Party highlighted Stalin's ruthless streak. 'Stalin', which means man of steel, was a well-chosen alias adopted by the young Joseph Djugashivili to help avoid detection by the Tsar's secret police. Yet it was Stalin's qualities as an organiser, as well as his willingness to obey orders that brought him to the attention of Lenin. Stalin's promotion to the Central Committee of the Bolshevik Party helped provide it with a more practical and proletarian image than that of the intellectuals who made up the majority of the party's leadership. As one of Lenin's most loyal followers Stalin was rewarded with the position of Commissar for Nationalities after the October Revolution. The rivalry between Stalin and Trotsky seems to have emerged at this time when they came into conflict over military matters – Stalin having some responsibility over the military in the Caucasus region while Lenin was in charge of the Red Army.

Trotsky may have shared Stalin's tendency to authoritarianism but in other respects they were completely different characters. Trotsky had been a brilliant student. Born near Odessa, he studied mathematics at the town's university and it soon became obvious that he had a formidable intellect and was a superb orator. He was at his best when dealing with a crisis. His thorough and energetic preparation and execution of the October Revolution as well as his work in organising the Red Army during the civil war showed these qualities. But there was another side to Trotsky. He was a Jew by birth and his 'Jewishness' did lead to some prejudice against him within the party. His arrogance and aloofness, while making him unpopular with the party, also led to a lack of judgement on occasions. Trotsky was not a team player and made little attempt to endear himself to others. His main qualities were, by his own admission, 'unsociability, individualism and aristocratism'. His attitude, that it was only he who held in his mind the overall picture of actions and their implications and let others concern themselves with details, did not go down well with his colleagues. Trotsky had been a Menshevik until the summer of 1917 and his late conversion was seen as evidence of his opportunism as well as his lack of commitment to the party. His lack of support in the party was shown when he came tenth in elections to the Central Committee at the tenth Party Congress in 1921. Many Bolsheviks wondered whether Trotsky was a man of the party or was working to his own agenda. These concerns were to become more significant after 1917 with the Bolsheviks' growing obsession with the fate of their revolution. An examination of the course of the earlier French Revolution showed the possible dangers. Out of the French Revolution Napoleon Bonaparte had emerged as dictator. Would the Bolshevik Revolution suffer the same fate? Many Bolsheviks were concerned that a potential Bonaparte could be lurking in the party and they assumed it would be a charismatic figure with grand visions and army connections. Trotsky's personality and background made him, in the minds of many Bolsheviks, the most likely candidate for this role and these suspicions created a degree of hostility to Trotsky from within the party.

The differences in personality between Stalin and Trotsky were to be highlighted in the manner in which each individual adapted to and made use of the situation that arose in 1924 with Lenin's death.

2. The situation in 1924

This was somewhat confused by the fact that Lenin had given no clear indication of what the power structure should be after he had gone. This resulted in an uncertain atmosphere, which worked to Stalin's advantage. Stalin had started to lay the foundations for his rise to power while Lenin was still alive, using the weaknesses in the central power structure caused by Lenin's illness to his own advantage. He drew on his powers as General Secretary of the party to gather information. Even Lenin's private home was bugged in order to keep Stalin supplied with information. While Lenin was recovering from his series of strokes at Gorky it was Stalin who provided the link between the leader and the Politburo. After his third stroke in March 1923 Lenin lost all powers of speech except monosyllables such as 'vot vot' (here, here). In this situation Stalin was in a powerful position. Above all, Stalin recognised that the main focus of power was not the government but the party's Politburo. The growth in the scope and responsibility of the state had made some positions more important than others and as the party had developed its roles in the administration of the state it was the party structure which grew in power. The head of the party structure was the General Secretary and in 1924 it was Stalin who held this post.

3. Stalin's positions within the party

By 1924 Stalin had gained not only useful influence within the party but also invaluable experience of how the party functioned. As Commissar for Nationalities, a post he held from 1917 until 1923, Stalin was in charge of the officials in the various republics outside Russia. In 1919 Stalin was also appointed as Liaison Officer between the Politburo and the Orgburo (the party's bureau of organisation), a post which allowed Stalin to monitor party personnel and policy. In the same year Stalin was made Head of the Workers' and Peasants' Inspectorate, a wide-ranging post which involved overseeing the work of all government departments. The key position, however, was that of General Secretary of the party, which Stalin gained in 1922. This post gave him access to a wealth of information on party members. There were few Politburo members not under his surveillance. More importantly, the post of General Secretary gave Stalin the power of patronage: he had the right to appoint people to party positions and this provided him with a means of promoting his own supporters to key positions. As time went by more and more party officials owed their loyalty to Stalin. As the 1920s progressed those who opposed Stalin were removed from the Politburo and replaced by Molotov, Kalinin and Voroshilov, all cronies of Stalin. Kirov was made head of the party in Leningrad in 1926 when Stalin wanted a loyal supporter to replace the out-of-favour Zinoviev. When it came to votes on party issues, Stalin could always outvote and outmanoeuvre his opponents. The levers of power were in Stalin's hands. In contrast, Trotsky remained Commissar for War until 1925, a position which provided him with useful links with the army but less influence in the party structure as a whole. In fact, as Commissar for War, Trotsky had been made responsible for the requisitioning of grain during the civil war and this had gained him little support among the rural population.

Although Stalin did not create the party structure, he was able to use it to his advantage. His capacity for thoroughness in administration enabled him to prosper in this set-up. He had gained the position of General Secretary because others had turned it down as being too uninteresting. However, it suited Stalin's skills and provided a useful cover for any ambitions he might have. Some party members nicknamed Stalin 'Comrade Card-Index', a reference to his willingness to undertake routine administrative tasks. Sukhanov referred to Stalin as the 'grey blur', a good administrator but someone who lacked personality. These comments may seem like criticisms of Stalin's qualities but in the circumstances of 1924 and with the party's fear of a Bonaparte figure emerging, these qualities were a positive advantage.

4. Structural changes in the party
Between 1923 and 1925 the party increased its membership by launching the 'Lenin Enrolment'. This enhanced Stalin's power within the party. The aim of this membership drive was to increase the number of true proletarians in the party ranks. The campaign resulted in a flood of new members who were largely poorly educated and politically naïve. They may have seen the party as an opportunity to further their career and escape from the working class, certainly many of these new members made successful careers in the party structure. It is clear that these new members saw the party as a source of privileges and that retaining these privileges depended upon their loyalty to those who had allowed them into the party. As General Secretary, it was Stalin who was responsible for supervising the 'Lenin Enrolment' and it greatly extended his influence in the party. He could provide party officials with better living quarters, additional food rations and trips abroad to recuperate from illness. Stalin's humble background may well have helped him in his identification of the needs and demands of these new members and, in the power struggle which followed, Stalin was careful to ensure his views echoed those of the rank and file in the party.

5. Lenin's funeral
One obvious opportunity which Stalin had for presenting himself to the party was at the funeral of Lenin, an occasion which showed both Stalin's skills in manipulating events and Trotsky's lack of judgement and tactical

weaknesses. Although the Politburo had declared itself a collective leadership on the death of Lenin, manoeuvring behind the scenes was already evident. Stalin gained the advantage of being the one who delivered the oration at Lenin's funeral. This enabled him to present himself as the chief mourner and also gave him an opportunity to highlight his intention of continuing the work of Lenin. In contrast, Trotsky did not even turn up at the funeral. The reasons for his absence are still unclear but the excuse he gave was that Stalin had not informed him of the date. This was a somewhat lame excuse and it comes across as rather unconvincing. Whatever the reasons for his absence, it was a serious tactical mistake as it raised doubts about Trotsky's respect for Lenin. Trotsky also missed an opportunity to undermine Stalin by his refusal, along with Zinoviev, to publish Lenin's Testament.

6. The 'Lenin legacy'

In the atmosphere of hero worship, which was prevalent at the funeral, Stalin was able to present himself as the heir to the 'Lenin legacy'. Lenin quickly became an almost god-like figure to the party and Stalin, from his early experience in a theological seminary, was aware of the power of religious symbolism. To present oneself as the worthy continuer of the Lenin legacy was to enhance greatly Stalin's standing in the Party. Stalin emphasised the need to apply the ideas of Lenin and this carried more weight from someone like Stalin who seemed to have few ideas of his own. Stalin inaugurated the Lenin Institute to further the study of Lenin's works and gave a series of lectures on Leninism at the Communist University in Moscow. Trotsky, on the other hand, completely misjudged this mood and launched an attack on Lenin's New Economic Policy in his essays *Lessons on October* (1924).

7. Trotsky's attack on party bureaucracy

As well as attacking the policies of Lenin, Trotsky also criticised the growing bureaucracy in the party. With this growth Trotsky saw the party losing its revolutionary spirit. These comments were to increase his unpopularity. To Trotsky the bureaucracy had grown to the point where it was in danger of becoming the master rather than the servant of the people. The bureaucracy had, of course, grown in size under Lenin and as such Trotsky's comments could again be seen as a criticism of Lenin's work. As the party was now the main vehicle for social mobility in the Soviet Union, its members were anxious to protect the privileges that they had gained through the party. Trotsky's attack on party bureaucracy was therefore seen as a threat and as a result there was little support for Trotsky in the party. When these criticisms came to a head in early 1924 Trotsky faced opposition from a triumvirate of Stalin, Zinoviev and Kamenev. Trotsky's support was confined to a few cells in the party, the universities and the Red Army. The triumvirate on the other hand could set in motion most of the party apparatus in its favour due to Stalin's influence as General Secretary. When delegates to the Thirteenth Party Conference were elected in 1924 Trotsky's supporters were small in number. Trotsky made little attempt to organise himself and his supporters within the party. He felt that inter-party squabbling was beneath him and his arrogance again became a problem. He made few efforts to win friends. Stalin's tactics reaped more rewards, however. The rallying of support in the party through his influence as General Secretary was a tactic which he would repeat on several occasions when faced with opposition. Trotsky's actions were also limited by Lenin's rule against factionalism, *On Party Unity*. This provided Stalin with another weapon he could use against his opponents when differences arose over ideology and policy.

In 1926 Stalin was in a position to deal effectively with Trotsky. The levers of power were in Stalin's hands and even though Trotsky had, in the ideological debate, improved his position by allying himself with both Zinoviev and Kamenev, Stalin was able to gather together support within the party in order to defeat Trotsky's opposition. By 1929 Trotsky was not only no longer in the party but also no longer in the Soviet Union, having been expelled and sent to Alma-Ata in central Asia before being exiled abroad on Stalin's orders. Stalin had shown himself to be highly skilled in manipulating the situation after 1924. His personality was better suited to political manoeuvring than that of Trotsky but ultimately it was Stalin's position within the party structures and the manner in which he aligned himself with the attitudes of party members that sealed his victory. To the rank and file membership Stalin represented a safer future for them and the revolution than the more 'dangerous' figure of Trotsky. It was perhaps not just Stalin who was successful but also the system itself.

HOW IMPORTANT WERE IDEOLOGICAL DIFFERENCES IN STALIN'S RISE TO POWER?

The events which saw the defeat not just of Trotsky and the Left but also of the Right of the party leadership were centred on differences over ideology. These differences were not, however, deep and irreconcilable divisions, but they did provide opportunities to rid the party leadership of people who were opposed to Stalin. The role of Stalin in these debates does, in itself, illustrate his tactics of manoeuvring himself into a dominant position while outmanoeuvring and isolating his opponents.

The defeat of the Left

All the Bolshevik leaders were committed to the building of socialism in the Soviet Union and saw that industrialisation and urbanisation were the keys to achieving this. On this they were all agreed. The differences arose over the methods and speed of this development and the division between the Left and the Right of the Communist Party was centred on a difference of emphasis on two main issues: the future of the NEP and the call for 'Permanent Revolution'.

The future of the NEP. This was an issue which quickly came to the fore after Lenin's death. Lenin, himself, had viewed the NEP as a temporary measure needed to get the economy going again after the privations of the civil war and to win over the peasantry to the Bolshevik Revolution. Lenin had, however, given little indication of how long this temporary phase should last. The Left saw the NEP, with its emphasis on elements of capitalist free enterprise, as a betrayal of the aims of the revolution. The compromise with the peasantry, allowing them the right to sell surpluses at market for a profit, was seen as holding back the move towards a true proletarian state based on socialist principles. The Right on the other hand, saw the NEP as a legitimate policy which should be retained as long as it worked; in other words, so long as the nation's food needs were met.

In this debate Trotsky, Zinoviev and Kamenev put forward the views of the Left, forming the so-called 'United Opposition' in 1926. The Right was centred on Bukharin, Rykov and Tomsky. The differences between Left and Right were outlined in debates between the economist Preobrazhensky, a supporter of the United Opposition, and Bukharin from the Right. Preobrazhensky, from the viewpoint of an economist, argued that resources such as food would have to be extracted from the peasantry to support any industrialisation. Bukharin, from a political viewpoint, saw the importance of the alliance between the workers and peasants, which Lenin's NEP had created, in ensuring the survival of the regime. Where did Stalin stand in this debate? The fact that he did not participate in this debate led most to conclude that he supported his old ally Bukharin.

The difference over the future of the NEP was, it must be said, merely a difference of emphasis. The attitude of nearly all of the Bolshevik leaders was that the NEP would not last indefinitely. Few had any enthusiasm for the Nepmen, those private traders who were seen to have gained from the NEP. The Bolsheviks were also in agreement in their suspicions about the kulaks, the more prosperous peasants who seemed to represent a capitalist class of profiteers undermining the revolution. What brought the differences over the NEP to the forefront was the unexpectedly rapid industrial growth of 1924–25. This led to a wave of optimism that the revolution could, perhaps, move forward to socialism and the NEP could be ditched rather more quickly than had previously been anticipated. The Left partly represented this optimism. Yet in the political manoeuvring of the mid-1920s the issue was confused by the way these policy differences were linked to questions of party loyalty. To call for a hasty abandonment of the NEP could be interpreted as a move away from the work of Lenin and a wrecking of his legacy.

The call for 'Permanent Revolution'. The ideological debate also became tied to a questioning of loyalty through the issue of 'Permanent Revolution' put forward by Trotsky. The priority, according to Trotsky, was the need to spread worldwide revolution to secure the success of the Bolshevik takeover in Russia. Without this revolutionary zeal the party would succumb to conservative forces and the bureaucracy would lose sight of its original role of working on behalf of the proletariat and would operate in its own interests. The idea of Permanent Revolution caused division in 1925 when Stalin made his mark on policy direction by promoting the idea of 'Socialism in One Country'. It was already clear that the wave of world revolution that the Bolsheviks had hoped for after 1917 had failed to materialise. Communist uprisings in Germany, Hungary and even in Glasgow had all failed. The Soviet Union was on her own, surrounded by hostile states. Stalin's slogan of 'Socialism in One Country' was a recognition of this reality. It called for modernisation through industrialisation by using the resources of the Soviet Union. To many of the old Bolsheviks this was disturbing as it ignored a major aspect of traditional Marxist theory: the need for a revolution on a world scale to bring down capitalism. The focus of 'Socialism in One Country' was on the Soviet Union and carried undertones of nationalism and patriotism. Trotsky was thus provoked into an attack on Stalin's policy, which enabled Stalin to present himself as a true patriot. How could the Soviet Union survive in a hostile world unless it first strengthened its position by industrialisation? Promoting world revolution, Stalin argued, could be achieved only after the Soviet Union was on a secure footing; to do otherwise was seen as irresponsible. Again, this was an argument over priorities rather than irreconcilable divisions but it enabled Stalin to portray Trotsky as both disloyal and irresponsible. Trotsky's call for world revolution was similar to that of the Mensheviks, a point Stalin made and, given Trotsky's Menshevik connections before the revolution, this again raised suspicions about whether Trotsky was a true Bolshevik Party man.

The formation of the United Opposition in 1926 gave Trotsky a focus for organising his position. Yet his alliance with Zinoviev and Kamenev was an uneasy and unconvincing one due to their past disagreements and they made little attempt to organise mass support for the Left's argument. Stalin was therefore able to defeat the United Opposition by exploiting their divisions and using his power as General Secretary to deliver the votes needed to defeat them. They were expelled from the Politburo and either demoted or sent into internal exile.

Nicolai Bukharin.

The defeat of the Right

The defeat of the Left Opposition did not end the debate over the future of economic policy and during the winter of 1927–28 the party leadership found itself once again divided over this issue as Stalin prepared to launch the first Five-Year Plan. Rather than a deep ideological division, the disagreement was over the pace of industrialisation. All of the Bolshevik leadership saw industrialisation as a necessary part of the consolidation of socialism and with it the Communist Party itself but divisions occurred over the role of the peasantry in this. In the absence of foreign capital how could the Soviet Union raise the resources needed to support large-scale industrialisation? The peasants would have to produce the food surpluses needed to support the growth in industry and with it the growth of towns. The Left had believed that the only way to do this was by force. The Right preferred a policy of persuasion, arguing that the use of force could actually cause food production to decline because of opposition from the peasantry. In early 1928, within months of the defeat of the Left, the proposals for the Five-Year Plan led to the emergence of a Right Opposition group which began to argue the case of the Right for a continuation of the framework introduced by the NEP and for any economic targets to be kept low so as to avoid the need for force in ensuring they were met. The leaders of the Right in the Politburo were Tomsky, the trade union leader; Rykov, who was the official head of the Soviet Government; and Bukharin, the editor of the communist newspaper *Pravda* and a distinguished economic theorist.

So why did Stalin suddenly become convinced that the only way forward was to impose industrialisation on the country?

At one level Stalin's change of view on the NEP and industrialisation can be seen as evidence of his use of political manoeuvring and opportunism to strengthen his own position in the leadership rather than as a genuine ideological shift. After getting rid of the Left he then adopted their policies in order to remove the Right. This view is perhaps rather cynical. It must be remembered that Stalin had largely stayed out of the earlier debate between Preobrazhensky and Bukharin over the future of the NEP and instead of changing his views from the Right to the Left, Stalin may well have been undecided. The conflict with the Left was also intrinsically linked to Stalin's power struggle with Trotsky: it was not ideology which provided the dominant division.

There are other factors which may well have forced Stalin to reconsider his policies. In 1927 there was a great deal of anxiety over an impending attack by the capitalist powers during which the peasants started to hoard their produce and shortages occurred in the industrial towns. It became clear to Stalin that the peasants were a major factor in holding back the industrial development of the Soviet Union. Without an increase in food production, further industrialisation could not be supported. He was also aware of a growing disillusionment among the party rank and file over the course of the revolution. The Nepmen, kulaks and 'bourgeois experts' who had survived due to the compromises of the NEP were the target of their frustration. This dissatisfaction was building up in the party and Stalin saw the potential of aligning himself with these views in order to strengthen his own position. Rapid industrialisation would provide an opportunity to sweep away the remnants of the old system and move to socialism. Thus, Stalin was reacting to trends and attitudes within the party and differences in ideology provided an opportunity to defeat the Right.

The position of the Right was weakened by Bukharin's refusal to try to build up an organised faction within the party. He was, no doubt, aware of the penalties associated with faction building that had been used against Trotsky. Bukharin's sense of loyalty meant that this debate was carried out behind closed doors and there was no direct appeal to the party members for support. The Right's power was based around the Moscow party organisation – led by Uglanov – and the Central Council of Trade Unions – led by the Politburo member, Tomsky. Both Uglanov and Tomsky were removed from their positions in the autumn of 1928.

By early 1929 the Right Opposition in the Politburo was identified by name and all were removed from their posts except Rykov, who remained Head of the Government until 1930.

The Right, like the Left, had been defeated by Stalin's use of the party organisation and structures. At face value the party divisions had been over issues of ideology but these differences should not be over-exaggerated. They were differences of emphasis and priority rather than irreconcilable splits. It is important to remember that the debate over the future direction of the revolution was taking place in the context of a struggle for power and, in this situation, differences in ideological emphasis gave Stalin the opportunity to magnify divisions and remove those who stood in his way. The collective leadership, which had been declared in 1924 at the death of Lenin, was no more, Stalin had whittled away at the power and positions of his other main rivals until, by early 1929, he was in a dominant position. He was now free to implement the Five-Year Plan and other policies unhindered.

HISTORICAL INTERPRETATIONS

Historians have found the issue of Stalin's rise to power difficult to explain. It involved a complex sequence of events in which it has not been easy to discern Stalin's position and motives in the constant struggle for power. Nonetheless, a range of factors has been identified which explain Stalin's rise to power and although no historian would suggest one single factor was responsible for the rise of Stalin, historians have differed in terms of which factor they see as the most important. Consequently different schools of historians have placed the emphasis on varying factors, often depending on the underlying philosophical principles of the historical school to which the individual historian belongs.

The Liberal School
Historians of the liberal school have focused on the role of individuals and their personalities. According to this view the main factors in Stalin's rise to power were his personal qualities. To liberal historians Stalin is seen as having grit, determination, shrewdness, craftiness and, of course, cruelty. This view has been presented in works such as B D Wolfe's *Three who made a Revolution* (1974) and in Robert Conquest's psychological portraits of Stalin in *Stalin* (1991) as well as R Tucker's *Stalin as Revolutionary 1879–1929: A Study in History and Personality* (1974). Both Conquest and Tucker highlight Stalin's ruthlessness and double-dealing. They focus on the way in which Stalin deceived opponents, manipulated the situation after the death of Lenin and manipulated ideology for his own benefit. According to this approach,

Stalin's actions were merely devices to get rid of his opponents and make himself the dictator.

By highlighting the role of personality, the liberal school also provides an explanation of why the other Bolshevik leaders were unable to take advantage of the situation. The weaknesses of Stalin's opponents can be put down to deficiencies in their characters. Zinoviev is often presented as an unsavoury careerist, Kamenev as a politician without any coherent goal and Bukharin as politically shortsighted. These defects were crucial in their failure to use the situation after 1924 and to deal effectively with Stalin: no one was a match for the General Secretary. One major weakness which the Bolshevik leaders shared was in underestimating Stalin. In this respect, Zinoviev, Kamenev and Bukharin made the same mistake as Lenin, who only realised Stalin's true character when he was ill and it was too late to rectify the situation.

The other personality was, of course, Trotsky who, according to the liberal school, made tactical mistakes. His arrogance and indifferent personality also led him to underestimate Stalin as the 'grey blur' and 'outstanding mediocrity'. Trotsky's failure to organise his supporters and his absence at Lenin's funeral are emphasised as examples of his tactical failures.

When compared to the other Bolshevik leaders Stalin can be seen as the strongest personality, and therefore it is the role of personality that is highlighted by the liberal school to explain Stalin's rise to power. This approach is usually adopted in political biographies of Stalin where the focus is inevitably on the individual. The critical approach adopted by this school is largely due to the type of sources used. The liberal school tended to rely on sources from émigrés, many of whom had suffered at first hand from Stalin's actions. This seemed good evidence to support the underlying principle that the intentions of individuals do matter in the process of historical change. This intentionalist approach found some agreement with the school of Soviet writers which emerged after 1930.

The Soviet School before 1985

After 1930 Soviet writers presented a view of the rise of Stalin that also focused on the role of personality but in a more positive light. When Stalin was still alive it was dangerous to do otherwise. History was turned into **hagiography** as Stalin was praised as the leader who had saved socialism both from Trotsky and his supporters and from the Right Deviationists such as Bukharin. This view was presented by G F Alexandrov in *Joseph Stalin: A Short Biography* (1947) who stated 'Foremost in the attack on the party were Trotsky, that arch enemy of Leninism, and his henchmen'. E Yaroslavsky went even further in *Landmarks in the Life of Stalin* (1942) by stating 'Long may he live and

KEY TERM

Hagiography
Writing which glorifies its subject in an uncritical manner.

flourish, to the dismay of our enemies and to the joy of all working people – our own, dear Stalin.' This was clearly not a balanced account of Stalin's personality but it did represent the official viewpoint until the mid-1950s when Khrushchev succeeded Stalin and introduced his policy of destalinisation. Khrushchev was more critical of Stalin and his 'errors' and this was reflected in the historiography which came out of the Soviet Union. When Brezhnev replaced Khrushchev as Soviet leader in 1964 destalinisation was slowed down and Stalin was ignored rather than criticised. This remained the general view in Soviet history books written thereafter until Gorbachev opened up the debate again after 1985.

Russian writers since 1985

When Gorbachev implemented his policy of **Glasnost** in 1985 the greater openness it fostered had an enormous influence on how Soviet writers could look at the past. Gorbachev had asked for ideas on how the socialist system could be improved and as a result there was a lot of criticism of the system Stalin had developed. By the Party Conference of 1988 most journalists and intellectuals openly rejected Stalin's repressive dictatorship as a betrayal of the original spirit of the revolution. It was convenient for many Russians to blame all the sins of the regime on one person rather than the system itself, but as the Russian people moved towards a rejection of the Soviet system in its entirety the focus moved to Lenin and the establishment of the regime as the original sin. The rise of Stalin was seen as a result of the system created by Lenin and the attitudes and structures that developed with it. This view occurs in the works of Dmitri Volkogonov (1990; 1996) and mirrors, although from a different perspective, recent views from western historians.

The Trotskyist approach

As a major player in the struggle with Stalin, Trotsky's viewpoint has a lot of value to the historian but he was obviously not an objective commentator. As someone who suffered at the hands of Stalin, and ultimately lost his life to one of Stalin's agents, he had an axe to grind.

Trotsky's perspective was a Marxist one. He saw Russia as not ready for revolution due to its economic backwardness. As a result the revolution deteriorated, the working class being too small in number to transform it into a true democratic dictatorship of the proletariat. Instead, according to Trotsky, it became a party-state machine of bureaucrats which ruled in its own interests. Stalin's success was due to his being a product of the circumstances caused by the NEP; his actions were part of the process whereby the bureaucrats strengthened their position at the expense of the revolution. In Trotsky's own words: 'All the worms are crawling out of the upturned soil of the manured revolution'.

Trotsky's views were presented through books written while he was in exile and include *My Life* (1931) and *The Revolution Betrayed* (1937). Despite his obvious bias, Trotsky was able to present his argument, making use of valuable inside knowledge. His recollection of some events is rather selective and some points made are unconvincing; for example, the reason given for not attending Lenin's funeral is weak. Nonetheless, for all its limitations, Trotsky's argument has formed the basis of much of the revisionist work which has moved the emphasis away from the personality of Stalin to the structures and social context within which he operated.

The Structuralist approach

In the West the standard liberal view of the importance of Stalin's personality was challenged in the 1960s and 1970s by the structuralist approach. This view sees Stalin's rise to power as a triumph of the party organisation rather than of the individual. Historians who have adopted this approach have emphasised the centralisation of policy into the hands of the party. The party administration started to replace the government and administration replaced politics. This was a direct response to the growth of responsibilities taken on by the party as the machinery of the state was enlarged. In this structure, the centre of power became the Secretariat and, at its head, the General Secretary. It was therefore Stalin's position as General Secretary which was the key factor in his rise to power due to the enormous authority and influence attached to this role. Attention has been drawn to the trend of appointment replacing election within the party and this was a crucial factor in explaining why Stalin was able to win votes if not arguments because the party officials had often been put in place by his own orders as General Secretary.

Structuralist historians have indicated that Stalin's power was aided by the attitudes and ethos that developed within the party. The old values of the tsarist bureaucracy of lack of initiative, boorishness and respect for authority were reinforced in the new system not only by the use of ex-tsarist civil servants but also by purges which removed those who showed signs of disloyalty.

The structuralist viewpoint was presented by E H Carr in *The Bolshevik Revolution* (1950–53), O A Narkiewicz in *The Making of the Soviet State Apparatus* (1970) and L Schapiro in *The Origins of the Communist Autocracy* (1965). The value of the structuralist approach is that it draws attention to the structures within which Stalin, and his rivals, had to operate. The increase in available sources from the Soviet archives since the mid-1980s has enabled historians to look in more depth at the working of the party structures, especially at lower and regional levels. This trend has led to some structuralists developing their ideas in a slightly different direction by looking at the history of the party.

The Party History approach

This approach has built on the structuralist standpoint by examining trends within the Bolshevik Party, looking at the growth of the party and its structures under Lenin. In *What is to be done?* (1902) Lenin had stated that the working class could never carry through a revolution unaided. It would require an organised party to guide the revolution on behalf of the workers. This party would, according to Lenin, need to be organised, disciplined and centralised. Historians looking at the party's history have seen these qualities present since October 1917 and even before it seized power. They draw attention to Lenin's lack of tolerance when faced with the development of factions. Thus, according to this viewpoint Stalin was the legitimate heir of Lenin in that Stalin's rise was based on a party structure that Lenin had put in place and that Stalin had merely used.

The party history approach has been put forward by G Gill in *The Origins of the Stalinist Political System* (1990) and R Service in *The Bolshevik Party in Revolution: a Study in Organisational Change 1917–23* (1979). As well as making use of a wider range of sources this approach has been valuable in highlighting the elements of continuity in Bolshevik history.

The ideological approach

The more traditional view that Stalin was an evil schemer, as presented by the orthodox liberal school in the West, has also been challenged by those historians who see matters of ideology and the debate over the NEP as more than a disguise for Stalin's personal ambition. This viewpoint has been put forward by E H Carr (1979) and M Lewin in *Political Undercurrents in Soviet Economic Debates from Bukharin to the Modern Reformers* (1974). Historians adopting the ideological approach stress that the struggle between Trotsky and Stalin was over the crucial issue of the future direction of the revolution. This debate was set within the context of Lenin's retreat to the NEP and his failure to lay down clearly an indication of the life-span of the NEP. To historians of this school the Left's view that the NEP should be ditched as soon as possible can be seen as a recipe for civil war between the peasants, who had gained under the policy, and the industrial workers who resented the concessions of the NEP. The Right's desire to maintain the NEP could, on the other hand, be seen as likely to lead to a restoration of capitalism due to its toleration of private enterprise. Stalin's position in this debate was therefore not that of an opportunist but of a practical politician balancing between two extremes. Thus, Stalin was prepared to keep the NEP while it worked but when it got into crisis he saw rapid industrialisation as the solution. Stalin's attack on Trotsky's notion of Permanent Revolution could also be seen as the action of a practical politician worried about the possibility of the Soviet Union getting involved in a war it was ill-equipped to fight.

The ideological approach does draw attention to the issues around which the struggle for power centred but many historians of the liberal school criticise it for underestimating the role of personality and for presenting Stalin in too positive a light. Liberal historians who saw communism as a threat to the western system of liberal democracy preferred the image of a Soviet leader who was unprincipled and manipulative. The ideological approach has, however, received support from some of the revisionist work undertaken since the mid-1980s.

The Revisionist School

With the release of more historical sources from the mid-1980s onwards, the traditional views of the rise of Stalin have been challenged with the emergence of revisionist historians. The main thrust of the revisionists has been an examination of social factors and changes in cultural attitudes and values. The wealth of sources available since *Glasnost* has made this area of study much more viable. Sheila Fitzpatrick in *The Civil War as a Formative Experience* (1985) stresses the expansion of the party during the civil war and how this affected its attitudes. The civil war led to a need for authoritarianism and discipline in the party in order to ensure the effective use of resources during the war. The new members who joined the party at this time took on the military values which were reinforced by the war situation.

Social change has also been highlighted in other studies, such as W Chase's *Workers, Society and the Soviet State 1918–1929* (1987), which examine the Lenin Enrolment of 1924 and have emphasised how it transformed the composition of the party. In order to control this huge growth in membership, obedience rather than debate was encouraged. This trend worked to the advantage of Stalin who, as General Secretary, controlled the party bureaucracy. With the influx of new members the gap between the rank and file of the party and the leadership increased. This was a concern which Stalin recognised and the attacks on both Trotsky and the Right of the party can be seen as attempts to get the party leadership the support of party members. Trotsky's criticism of the growth of the party's bureaucracy was a threat to the newly gained privileges of its members; Stalin's campaign against Trotsky was therefore popular with the party rank and file. By attacking the Right and moving away from the NEP, Stalin was able to gain support from the industrial workers and party members who wished to see an end to those remnants of the old system, such as the Nepmen, who posed a possible threat to their position.

The value of these revisionist studies is in their use of social history to examine events from the perspective of the ruled rather than the rulers. The revisionist school is, however, criticised because it tends to present Stalin as a puppet of social forces in the party rather than someone who had control over events. In this sense the revisionist approach challenges the intentionalist assumption that individuals do matter in the process of historical change.

CONCLUSION

Although historians from the liberal school focus on the personality of Stalin, it is evident that Stalin's personality cannot be divorced from the world he operated in. The structuralists and revisionist approaches have highlighted the context within which Stalin had to work. This context included important changes which were taking place in the party and society in general. Stalin may not have possessed the power to control events which was assumed by the orthodox liberal school but he was able to tap into values and attitudes generated by the circumstances which had surrounded Bolshevik rule since 1917. The greater availability of sources since the opening up of archives after 1985 has provided historians with the ability to examine a wider range of factors with greater validity.

Summary of interpretations of the rise of Stalin

Key issue: How important was the role of personality in the rise of Stalin?

The Liberal School
VIEW:
• focuses on the importance of individual personalities
• sees Stalin as a manipulator who rose to power by deceiving his opponents

WHY:
• relates to the underlying philosophy of the intentionalist approach to history – individuals can influence the course of history
• heavy reliance on the evidence of those who suffered at the hands of Stalin
• put forward by liberal historians in the West to whom communism was intrinsically evil

VALUE:
• draws attention to the role of Stalin and other individuals

---

The Soviet School before 'Glasnost' (1985)

VIEW:

- saw Stalin's role as being of some influence within the context of socio-economic forces highlighted by Marxist perspective

WHY:

- related to standard Soviet view based on Marxism
- positive/negative view of Stalin depending on Soviet leader in power at the time of publication: hagiography under Stalin, more critical under Khrushchev – both views for the propaganda purposes of the regime at the time

VALUE:

- highlights the importance of socio-economic changes leading to the rise of Stalin
- but view of Stalin related to political factors rather than evidence

Russian writers since 1985

VIEW:

- tend to see the rise of Stalin as an inevitable result of authoritarian trends in the party

WHY:

- related to greater freedom of views after *Glasnost*
- promoted by the rejection of the Soviet system and communism since 1991

VALUE:

- they present the view of those most affected by the legacy of Stalin
- make use of a lot of new material previously unavailable in the West

The Trotskyite School

VIEW:

- Stalin was a product of his circumstances. He represents a conservative reaction by bureaucrats sacrificing the revolution for their own interests

WHY:

- relates to Marxist approach of examining the importance of socio-economic change

VALUE:

- Trotsky experienced the rise of Stalin at first hand
- but his failure to defeat Stalin coloured his view

The Structuralist and Party History approaches

VIEW:

• see the rise of Stalin as a product of the structures of the party: the Party History Approach sees continuity in the structural framework of the party since Lenin

WHY:

• related to the challenge to the dominant liberal school in the West in the 1960s and 1970s

VALUE:

• focuses on the role of party structures in the rise of Stalin

The ideological approach

VIEW:

• emphasises the importance of ideology in Stalin's rise to power: Stalin driven by practical and ideological reasons not personal ambition

WHY:

• part of the challenge to the more critical view of Stalin as a schemer for personal power presented by the Liberal School

VALUE:

• focuses on ideology as a factor, moving attention away from western, stereotyped views of Stalin

The Revisionist School

VIEW:

• sees the rise of Stalin as due to social and cultural changes in the party membership: Stalin, the individual, is less important, merely representing social trends

WHY:

• relates to the increased use of sources available since *Glasnost* making social history more valid

VALUE:

• focuses on the influence of rank and file party members in shaping historical developments
• but downplays the role of Stalin

How did Stalin exercise political control?

The policies of collectivisation, the Five-Year Plans and the use of terror have resulted in much debate over Stalin's contribution to the development of the Soviet Union and communism in practice.

Stalin saw himself as the continuer of Lenin's work; someone who would ensure the achievements of Lenin were safeguarded from the attacks of counter-revolutionaries. This theme is evident in much of Stalin's work and was used to justify the nature of the Stalinist State.

WHAT WAS THE NATURE OF THE STALINIST STATE?

Lenin had made it clear that the move from capitalism to socialism would need to involve the creation of a Dictatorship of the Proletariat. This would be a temporary stage where the Bolshevik Party would take control of the reins of political and economic power on behalf of the proletariat. Once counter-revolutionaries had been dealt with, the State would not be needed. As society became based on co-operation, government would 'wither away'. This did not happen. Under Lenin the apparatus of state had increased and under Stalin this trend continued. Critics of Stalin have argued that instead of a Dictatorship of the Proletariat, governing on behalf of the workers, the Soviet Union was ruled by a personal dictatorship of Stalin.

WHAT EVIDENCE IS THERE FOR A PERSONAL DICTATORSHIP BY STALIN?

Stalin's leadership of the Soviet Union is often seen in terms of a personal dictatorship with many western historians focusing on the personality of Stalin as a determining force in the political structure of the USSR. This approach has drawn attention to the role of Stalin and his personality traits. He has been portrayed as a schemer with a lack of principle, who took action to strengthen his own position to ensure all power rested in his hands. The evidence for this lay in an examination of the methods used by Stalin to extend his control and dominance over the Communist Party.

Stalin's control over the Communist Party

In theory the Communist Party was a democratic institution, but in reality power was centralised in the hands of the party leadership. This had occurred during Lenin's leadership in response to the civil war. Strong central direction was needed in the face of severe threats from enemies. In the 1930s Stalin ensured this situation not only continued but was also enhanced.

Stalin had been General Secretary of the party since 1922 and had quickly learnt to appreciate the importance of this position within the emerging power structure. As the bureaucracy of the party continued to grow, the power of the General Secretary at its head increased. This was a trend that Lenin had been late to recognise, despite the warnings of Trotsky. Stalin used it to his advantage. In this respect, it could be argued that the seeds of Stalinism were sown by Lenin. Stalin had used his position to collect information on party members and to promote his own supporters within the party. Thus he was able to use the structures of the party to his own advantage. By placing his own supporters into positions within the party, he could outvote his opponents.

In 1924 the Politburo was made up of the following members: Bukharin, Zinoviev, Kamenev, Rykov, Tomsky, Trotsky and Stalin. By the end of 1930 Stalin was the only surviving member from this group, the others had been removed during the disputes over economic policy in the late 1920s. In their place were cronies of Stalin, such as Molotov, Voroshilov, Kaganovich and Kalinin. Thus, Stalin was able to ensure the Politburo was in agreement with his own policies. The use of terror against previous opponents sent clear messages to members of the Politburo about the likely consequences of opposing Stalin's wishes.

The key consequence of Stalin's methods was the failure of any political institution within the Soviet Union to gain any real power. All party and State institutions remained mechanisms for rubber-stamping official policies decided by the leadership, and this meant Stalin.

The Soviet Constitution of 1936

The working of the new Constitution of 1936 illustrates the failure of democratic institutions to develop despite official statements given by the government. At face value the Constitution seemed to be highly democratic. Stalin himself stated that 'the constitution of the USSR is the only thoroughly democratic constitution in the world'. Under the Constitution of 1936 every citizen in the USSR would be given the vote. This was an important change from the situation which had existed before 1936, where 'bourgeois' classes, such as the kulaks and priests, were excluded from the franchise. The Constitution stated that since these classes no longer existed there was no reason to deny any citizen the right to vote. Civil rights, including freedom of the press, religion and organisation were given under the Constitution. There was also a guarantee of employment that contrasted with the economic situation in many capitalist countries suffering from the effects of the Great Depression of the 1930s.

In practice the Constitution was a fraud. It listed restrictions on the rights of citizens and it was clear that nothing could threaten the dominance of the Communist Party. This was a measure of democracy imposed from above, and within the limits decided by the leadership. Only candidates from the Communist Party were allowed to stand in elections. The government announced that political parties in the democratic sense were a product of conflicts between classes which were generated by capitalism. The Soviet Union did not need more than one political party because these conflicts no longer applied to the Soviet Union. The start of the Great Terror in the following year illustrated the emptiness of many of the statements made in the Constitution.

The wording of the Constitution was directed at foreign governments as well as Soviet citizens. The 1930s had seen a growth in international tension with the rise of aggressive fascist states in Germany and Italy. The Soviet Union was aiming to show its own credentials against fascist states which had severely restricted human rights. In this respect the Constitution was designed to show Britain and France that the Soviet Union might make a satisfactory ally against Hitler. Needless to say, the Constitution was not taken too seriously either abroad or at home.

The failure of political institutions to develop any real power and influence was not caused by Stalin's actions alone. The situation inherited from Lenin had already established political bodies that were weak. Stalin's method of ruling merely continued to hold back the development of real decision-making outside the leadership. By 1924 the organisations of state had been subordinated by those of the party. The party structure was made up of the Party Congress, Central Committee and Politburo; each body being elected by members of the Communist Party. Yet in reality elections were controlled from above with those candidates that were favoured by the leadership automatically being voted into positions. This trend, which was evident before 1924, became fixed under Stalin. As the 1930s went on these institutions, including the Politburo, met less frequently as Stalin increased his control over them. In the 1920s the Politburo had met weekly but by the mid-1930s meetings were only held about nine times a year. Power became focused in sub-groups set up outside the Politburo over which Stalin could exercise firmer control. Stalin attended important meetings, where he would use the intimidating tactic of walking around the room while others spoke. There was a real fear that saying something disagreeable to Stalin would result in

The structure of the Communist Party

Politburo The key decision-making body, made up of an inner group of party leaders. Elected by the...

Central Committee In theory this was the key decision-making body in the party but its power declined rapidly after 1922. By 1934 it met only once every four months. Stalin increased the size of its membership which made discussing policy in detail difficult. Its decision-making function was exercised by the Politburo on its behalf. Elected by the . . .

Party Congress A body made up of representatives of local party branches. It discussed the general programme of the party. It declined in influence at the end of the 1920s and met only twice (1934 and 1939) between 1930 and 1952.

execution, this was the fate of General Rychagov who complained about the quality of Soviet aircraft.

The use of terror

Stalin's control over the party was in large part due to the use of terror and the threat of terror. Both were used against sections of the party and had the effect of ensuring loyalty to Stalin (or at least keeping possible opponents quiet). Opposition to Stalin's policies resulted in rather more than demotion or dismissal. The Left and Right Opposition were brought to trial and most were executed. The Great Terror saw the purging of local party officials as well as ex-members of the leadership. Stalin's instrument of terror was the NKVD, the secret police. Yet even the secret police were not safe. Yezhov replaced Yagoda in 1936. The latter was later executed (in 1938). It was useful for Stalin to ensure the terrorists themselves were kept in line. In this atmosphere of terror it is not surprising that the party was keen to follow the wishes of Stalin.

Although the use of terror can be seen as an integral part of Stalin's method of ruling, it was nothing new to the Communist Party. Lenin had exercised terror, especially during the civil war years, but it would be wrong to see Stalin's use of terror as a direct continuation of the work of Lenin. Lenin's use of terror was justified by the threat of counter-revolution during the difficult years of the civil war. This was not comparable to the situation facing Stalin in the 1930s. It is true that Stalin did justify terror as necessary because of the threat from 'class enemies' in the Soviet Union who were trying to sabotage the drive towards socialism. There is undoubtedly some truth in this justification, especially given the resistance to collectivisation. What is striking is that the Great Terror was launched in 1934 when the party's position seemed more secure. This would seem to indicate that Stalin was working to his own agenda, trying to secure his own personal position, rather than that of the party. In this sense, Stalin's use of terror differed from that of Lenin. What Stalin did owe to the work of Lenin was the attitude of many party members, developed during the civil war, that terror was an acceptable method of dealing with opponents both within and outside of the party.

In terms of the control exercised by Stalin over the party leadership there would seem to have been a trend towards personal dictatorship. It was a dictatorship reinforced by the use of terror. There were trends evident under Lenin that contributed to this situation: the growth of the bureaucracy, the failure of political institutions to develop and the use of terror. It is tempting to see Stalin's dictatorship as a product of the structures laid down after the Bolshevik Revolution of 1917. Yet it would be misleading to see Stalinism as the inevitable consequence of Leninism. There were important differences, the most significant being the move away from a Dictatorship of the Proletariat towards a personal dictatorship which served Stalin's own purposes. Nonetheless, it is also important to qualify the image presented by many western historians of the all-powerful Stalin.

What were the limits on Stalin's power?

Before one accepts the view of Stalin as an all-powerful dictator, it is important to consider the limits of his control.

Personal limits. Even if he had wished to, Stalin would not have been able to decide and control every issue. Stalin may have read long into the night but it was impossible for him to survey all the material necessary to keep on top of events in a country as large as the Soviet Union. This situation required prioritising to enable Stalin to focus on those issues of direct concern to himself.

Limits imposed from within the leadership. After the removal of the Left and Right Opposition groups during the debate over industrialisation, it is tempting to see the Politburo of the 1930s as a collection of Stalin's cronies. Individuals, such as Molotov, Kaganovich, Voroshilov and Kalinin, who were members of the Politburo, are often portrayed as dull, mediocre yes-men. There is undoubtedly a lot of truth in this view. Molotov remained loyal to Stalin even when his wife was imprisoned during the purges. There is, however, some evidence of the Politburo opposing Stalin's actions:

- In 1932, when Stalin wanted to execute **Ryutin**, who had denounced Stalin, the Politburo refused to agree and Ryutin was sentenced to ten years' in a labour camp instead.
- Stalin's ambitious targets for the second Five-Year Plan were considered too high for many both inside and outside the party. Even members of the Politburo felt the plan as it stood would result in chaos and opposition. Stalin was forced to accept a hurried redrafting of the plan with lower targets.
- Kirov, the popular leader of the party in Leningrad and member of the Politburo, may have represented a moderate faction within the leadership. He secured more votes than Stalin in the elections to the Politburo at the Party Congress of 1934. Did Kirov represent growing opposition to Stalin's policies? The evidence is unclear and the issue is confused still further by the possibility of Stalin being responsible for ordering his assassination later in the year.
- Some members of the Politburo expressed concern over Stalin's increasing use of brutality. Kuibyshev, head of Gosplan, may have expressed these concerns to Stalin but he died of a heart attack in 1935. Ordzhonikidze, Commissar for Heavy Industry, raised objections to the use of terror during meetings of the Politburo. Stalin tried to unnerve him by arresting and shooting his deputy. Ordzhonikidze cracked under the pressure: the cause of his death in 1937 was officially given as a heart attack but it was widely believed that he committed suicide. Other doubters included Voroshilov and Kalinin, both of whom became isolated in the Politburo.

Politics within the Soviet leadership remained a secretive process and evidence of relationships within the Politburo is difficult to find and interpret. The evidence available suggests the limits imposed on Stalin by members of the Politburo were minor, and diminished as the 1930s wore on, yet they showed that some dissatisfaction with Stalin did exist and could, on rare occasions, make itself known. Stalin surrounded himself with his cronies, but to serve Stalin's purpose they needed to be able to exercise the power Stalin had given them. This allowed some of Stalin's gang to develop their own agenda and Yezhov, head of the secret police, seems to have done this when implementing arrests and executions during the Great Terror.

Limits imposed from below. Recent evidence from social historians making use of sources that have become available since the collapse of the Soviet Union, has focused on the pressures exerted on Stalin and the leadership from rank and file party members. Party members were concerned about the continuing threat from enemies at home and abroad, and pushed for policies that would strengthen socialism in the USSR. Thus, Stalin was merely following the wishes of rank and file party members in bringing about the rapid industrialisation of the country.

Stalin and his cronies. Front row, left to right: Molotov, Kalinin, Voroshilov, Stalin, Kaganovich, Yezhov.

In 1930, Stalin's statement 'Dizzy with Success' can be seen as an attempt to bring over-zealous party officials, who were rapidly pushing through the policy of collectivisation, into line.

There is also evidence of the purges at local level resulting from conflict between local party members and regional authorities. Stalin may have directed the purges at the top but their scale at local level was determined by local pressures over which Stalin found it difficult to exercise control. Local studies have shown the situation on the ground, away from Moscow, to be far more chaotic than the traditional view of a dictatorship has indicated.

Although there were limits on Stalin's power, it is difficult to deny his importance in shaping events. Stalin was both a product of the situation inherited from Lenin and a force for using the opportunities presented in order to strengthen the system to his own advantage.

WHY DID THE GREAT TERROR OF THE 1930s TAKE PLACE?

Differing explanations for the Great Terror of the 1930s illustrate the debate over the degree to which Stalin was able to control events for his own purposes. To the foreign observer, the purges seemed to be evidence of the increasingly paranoid tendencies of Stalin as he saw threats to his own authority in even the most unlikely of places. Some communists who had fled the Soviet Union echoed Trotsky's accusation that this was part of Stalin's betrayal of the revolution. Yet it is too simplistic to blame the purges solely on Stalin's paranoia. The sheer scale of the purges in itself suggests a more complicated explanation is needed to understand them fully.

The role of Stalin's personality

The purges have been seen as evidence of Stalin's paranoia; as evidence of the personality defects of a dictator establishing his own ruthless power on the Soviet population. Psychological evidence of mental instability is difficult to prove but it is true that Stalin's behaviour became increasingly erratic as he got older. After the suicide of his second wife, Nadezhda, in 1932 Stalin became more and more reclusive, cut off from the world in his offices in the Kremlin and his dacha, a country villa outside Moscow. In these circumstances it would not be surprising if he became mentally unbalanced. Stalin saw opposition everywhere. He told Khrushchev: 'I trust nobody, not even myself'.

The assassination of Kirov in 1934, whether Stalin was responsible or not, was used as an excuse to strike against opponents. In the terror that followed Stalin personally signed many death warrants. He kept lists of victims in booklets and personally indicated the fate to be given to each by writing next to their name. Service (1997) attributes to Stalin personally the tactic of humiliating victims before their execution.

The historical roots:

- *Bolshevism.* Stalin's use of terror has been seen as a continuation of the trends established by Lenin after the Bolshevik Revolution of 1917. Lenin had built up a regime which was highly centralised around its leader and relied on terror to maintain itself in power. The Bolsheviks had always been a minority group in the Soviet Union and therefore it was necessary to use force in order for the regime to survive. This viewpoint has been argued by the liberal school of historians prominent in the West after 1945. They have seen all aspects of the Bolshevik regime in a negative light. Stalin, according to this view, grew out of the authoritarian tendencies in Bolshevism.
- *Russian traditions.* Rather than see Stalin's use of terror as a result of trends within Bolshevism, some historians have seen it within longer-term trends in Russian history. Thus, Stalin is seen as one in a long line of Russian despots imposing their will on the people by means of brutality. In this respect Stalin was similar to Ivan the Terrible and Peter the Great. This comparison has led to Stalin being referred to as a Red Tsar. It assumes there were conditions related to Russia's economic backwardness that made terror necessary in order to bring

about rapid change. This approach, sometimes referred to as 'Russia's Revenge' was popular with émigrés who had fled Russia during the 1920s but it has been criticised by more serious scholars as simplifying the situation by ignoring the different circumstances within which each leader had to rule.

Opposition to economic policies

The murder of Kirov can be seen as an excuse for Stalin to launch the purges but there were justifications for the use of terror in terms of dealing with the growth of opposition to economic policies.

The economic policies launched under the first Five-Year Plan and collectivisation had revealed opposition to the government's drive for a socialist utopia:

- The Left and Right Oppositions had attacked the economic policies of Stalin. The Left had criticised the concentration of power in Stalin's hands; the Right had expressed doubts about the forcible collectivisation of agriculture.
- Party officials such as Radek and Pyatakov had criticised the targets of the Five-Year Plans as unrealistic.
- The Red Army officers had been concerned about the impact of collectivisation on peasant morale in the armed forces. They had also established links with foreign countries under the secret treaties signed by the Soviet government with Germany. It was, perhaps, not surprising that suspicions regarding these links grew when Hitler started to adopt a more active foreign policy.

Thus, there was evidence that could be interpreted by communists, including Stalin, as a threat to the policies urgently needed if the revolution was to survive. Although these victims have often been seen in the West as merely scapegoats, sources from within the Soviet Union have shown a degree of real belief in the enemy within among the general population. Economic failures were often attributed to capitalist wreckers and if you were not one, then someone else must be the enemy.

For a Soviet nation in a state of alert against attack from both within and without there was perhaps a sense of urgency which justified the purges, for many rank and file party members, as necessary measures in order to safeguard the revolution.

Pressure 'from below'

The sheer scale of the purges suggests that there were factors at work other than Stalin himself. The purges at local level seemed to develop a life of their own as local communist officials were denounced by rank and file party members. John Arch Getty (1985) has drawn attention to the chaos that resulted from these denunciations. Using the evidence from the Smolensk Party Archive, which fell into American hands at the end of the Second World War, Arch Getty revealed the tension and struggle between party officials and the rank and file. These tensions led to the purge of large numbers of party members. In this situation Stalin and the leadership found it difficult to assert their authority.

CONCLUSIONS

From the perspective of Stalin there were clear justifications for the purges: all threats to his power and position were dealt with; loyalty had been enforced by fear. Although many of the death warrants had Stalin's name on them, there was more behind the purges than Stalin's wish to secure his own personal power. In terms of safeguarding the revolution during the difficult period of the upheavals of the Five-Year Plans and collectivisation, the use of terror kept the Soviet Union on track towards its goal of socialism. As a country in a virtual state of emergency against attack throughout the 1930s, there was a widespread fear of the enemy within. Since the early 1920s no opposition could exist outside the Communist Party, so it was not, perhaps, surprising that the enemy was now working within the party. This fear enabled the purges to snowball through a large degree of popular participation.

The excesses of the purges were in danger of undermining the progress of the revolution. They weakened the cohesion of the army and disrupted the economy by removing people with expertise and technical knowledge. Trotsky went further, criticising the purges as evidence of Stalin's betrayal of the revolution; that a personal dictatorship of Stalin had replaced a Dictatorship of the Proletariat. Yet Stalin could argue that the use of terror actually prevented a conservative reaction and kept the revolutionary spirit alive. The purges safeguarded not only the power of Stalin but also the position of the Communist Party. When a minority party, as the communists had always been, undertakes unpopular policies it needs terror to retain power. In this sense, and despite their appalling human cost, Stalin and his supporters could justify the purges as necessary measures to safeguard the revolution.

The role of Stalin – did Stalin preserve or destroy Bolshevism?

To commentators on the Right, Stalin and his policies have been seen as an inevitable consequence of the evils inherent in communism. Writers on the Left have been more positive about Stalin's achievements, although this has not been universal. Stalin's great rival, Trotsky, accused him of betraying the revolution by representing the interests of conservative, reactionary forces who hijacked the revolution for their own purposes. Stalin's supporters would argue that the policies of Stalin, far from destroying the revolution actually ensured its survival.

INTERPRETATIONS OF STALIN

The policies of collectivisation and the Five-Year Plans, coupled with large-scale use of terror and strict government control of society, have collectively been termed 'Stalinism'. This, in itself, implies that the role of Stalin was important, that Stalin was personally responsible for the developments which occurred in the 1930s. This viewpoint has been presented by writers from both the Left and the Right. Better access to sources since the fall of communism has enabled historians to examine the causes behind the policies in more detail, leading them often to qualify and challenge accepted standpoints on the role of Stalin.

Soviet historiography
The Soviet view under Stalin (1928–53). While Stalin was alive there could only be one view in the Soviet Union of the developments undertaken in the 1930s. With the government's rigid control over publications, Stalin was presented as an all-wise leader who saved the Soviet Union from its class enemies by the strict application of Marxist ideology. History itself became an instrument of social control, shaping attitudes and instilling the Soviet people with socialist ideology. In 1935 Stalin ordered an official history to be written, and in 1938 the *History of the All-Union Communist Party* was published. The book presented the official view of developments under Stalin and was to be used for teaching purposes. The *Short Course*, as it became known, was required reading for party members seeking promotion and a whole generation of Soviet citizens was educated in its views. The *Short Course* gave Stalin a prominent role in policy developments; as the continuer of Lenin's work, Stalin's role had been essential in saving the revolution. The victims of

Party youth members display loyalty to Stalin.

the purges of the 1930s were criticised as enemies of the state and Soviet people. This was less history than pure hagiography, with Stalin presented as a genius to be praised. The official history books of the 1930s were part of the process which created a cult of personality around the figure of Stalin, and an official biography of Stalin by G F Alexandrov followed in 1949. Alexandrov described Stalin as '. . . the genius, the leader and teacher of the party, the great strategist of Socialist revolution, helmsman of the Soviet State and captain of armies. His work is extraordinary for its variety; his energy truly amazing'.

It is, perhaps, too easy to criticise these official histories as a gross exaggeration of reality but there is evidence from sources released since 1985 that a substantial number of Russians, particularly industrial workers, saw Stalin and his policies as the creation of a dream which gave hope and equality. After the experiences of Tsarism, world war and civil war this was hardly surprising.

Trotsky and other Soviet émigrés. Given the strength of opposition to Stalin it is not surprising that those writers who had left the USSR challenged the official Soviet view. Russian émigrés, centred in Paris and the USA published a series of journals which revealed an uncensored account of the developments under Stalin. Many of these writers were Mensheviks who were highly critical of the Bolshevik Revolution and the course it had taken under Stalin. Important sources were released this way, including Bukharin's views on Stalin in an interview in Paris with the Menshevik historian Boris Nicolaevsky. Letters from Bukharin were also smuggled out of the USSR. They highlight Stalin's use of political intrigue, as well as Bukharin's sense of bitterness, and provided useful ammunition to those who wished to criticise Stalin and his policies.

The most prominent of the Soviet émigrés was Trotsky who, after his deportation from the Soviet Union, wrote a stream of anti-Stalinist works until silenced by one of Stalin's assassins in Mexico in 1940. Trotsky saw Stalin as a betrayer of the revolution, representing a 'Thermidorian', or conservative, reaction: using the power gained by the revolution for his own ends. *The Revolution Betrayed* (1937) was, however, also written to justify Trotsky's own actions and, as someone who had suffered at the hands of Stalin, it should be remembered that Trotsky had an axe to grind. Despite this, Trotsky's works provided a valuable insight and alerted the West to Lenin's testament. His unpublished papers and letters form the Trotsky Archive at Harvard University in the USA and have been available to western historians.

The Soviet view under Khrushchev (1953–64). When Khrushchev became leader of the Soviet Union in 1953 on the death of Stalin, he criticised some of Stalin's policies and introduced a policy of destalinisation. Stalin was accused of making 'errors' and deviating from the correct Marxist-Leninist line. The cult of personality and the use of terror, both of which Stalin had developed, were criticised. This change in emphasis was reflected in the history texts produced during Khrushchev's time as leader. The official history of 1938 was dropped from circulation and a committee of historians led by Boris Ponomaryov was appointed to prepare a new text. The resulting edition, published in 1959, systematically removed Stalin's name from any favourable connection and credit was given to the party and the people. The general thrust of the policies of Stalin, such as collectivisation and industrialisation, was not challenged and so a Marxist approach to the developments was retained while Stalin was made a scapegoat for mistakes and excesses. To have challenged the system itself would have been far too dangerous for both Khrushchev and the Communist Party.

Soviet historiography from Brezhnev to Gorbachev (1964–85).
Khrushchev's replacement as General Secretary in 1964 was Brezhnev. A conservative by temperament, Brezhnev was less keen than Khrushchev had been to denounce Stalin but had little intention of returning to full Stalinist policies. Brezhnev preferred to end the debate and there was little

discussion of it until Gorbachev became leader in 1985. Stalin was simply ignored in the history books produced in the USSR. It was as if Stalin, the famine of 1932 and the gulag had not existed. This viewpoint was presented in the *History of the USSR* (1981) by Y Kukushkin who stated: '. . . as time went by, all the achievements in socialist construction were erroneously credited to him (Stalin) and his personal leadership. This was a mistake as the crucial part played by the Soviet people and the Communist Party, the two decisive forces in the building of a new society, was thus relegated to the background'. This view was closer to the standard Marxist approach to history: that individuals are of little importance in the process of change compared to socio-economic forces. The reduction of Stalin's influence was not, however, a conclusion all Soviet writers could support.

Too many commentators in the West assume that all Soviet writers during the 1970s and 1980s adhered to the official line put forward by the government. While this view is largely true, there were notable exceptions. Dissidents, unhappy with the Soviet regime under which they were living, were able to write in the more relaxed atmosphere of the 1970s, even if they were restricted and found publishing their work difficult. Some, such as Sakharov and Solzhenitsyn, smuggled their writings out of the country for publication in the West. One important contributor to the debate on Stalin was R Medvedev, a dissident who lived in Moscow. His books were banned in the USSR but published abroad. *Let History Judge* (1971) gave no hint that Medvedev was not a communist. He saw Stalinism as a series of deviations and errors from the correct Marxist line and focused on the responsibility of Stalin, although he did not ignore the role of the party. According to Medvedev, Stalin's policies did have an element of mass support. Medvedev did not see Stalinism as a reason to reject the revolution as a whole and contested the idea that Stalinism was an inevitable consequence of the Bolshevik Revolution. He did, however, acknowledge the 'black shadow' cast by Stalin's policies. The chief value of Medvedev's work is the disclosure of information and testimony that would otherwise have been lost, yet his overall conclusion was similar to the standard line that Stalin was responsible for errors made.

Soviet historiography under Gorbachev (1985–91). Gorbachev, who became leader of the Soviet Union in 1985, represented a younger generation than those who had held the leadership since 1964. He was from the generation that had been heavily influenced by the ideas of Khrushchev; they believed that the Soviet system could be reformed to make communism more effective. Gorbachev's policies of *Glasnost* (openness) and *Perestroika* (economic restructuring) were part of this search for new ideas to reform the system. These policies involved a debate on the past as Gorbachev encouraged a 'Back to Lenin' view which saw Stalin's period of leadership as a drift away from the original aims of the revolution. To Gorbachev there were alternatives to the policies of Stalin, such as those of Bukharin, which would have taken the USSR towards communism.

In the new more relaxed atmosphere of *Glasnost* it became possible for Soviet writers to criticise Stalin, a trend evident in satirical magazines such as *Krokodil*. The movement unleashed by Gorbachev proved to be unstoppable and it was not long before writers started to ask questions about Lenin and the value of communism itself. These questions were to be raised not just by Russians but by the other national groups within the USSR. For the Ukrainians, Georgians and peoples of the Baltic States, criticising the Soviet system in its entirety was part of the wider political aim of breaking away from a Russian-dominated Soviet Union and reasserting their own national identity.

Russian writers since 1991. The collapse of the Soviet Union in 1991 led to a change from socialism towards a free market economy. In Russia this move was promoted by Boris Yeltsin, the Russian President. As capitalist economics were being applied in Russia a cultural revolution was needed to encourage the population to adopt new attitudes. Despite a reservoir of communist support among many of the older generation, it was easier for the new government to discredit the old Soviet system than to gain clear support for what should replace it. Western-style democracy needed time to gain support and consolidate its hold over the population.

The first serious biography of Stalin by a historian, as opposed to the rush of journalists who went into print after 1985, was that of Dmitri Volkogonov. His *Stalin: Triumph and Tragedy*, published in 1990, was the first part of a trilogy on the three important figures of the revolution. His biographies of Trotsky and Lenin followed in 1992 and 1996 respectively. Volkogonov's background in the Soviet army and his access to both army and party sources made his work particularly valuable. As a member of the intelligentsia who kept their heads down during the Brezhnev years, Volkogonov had been in a position to accumulate a vast amount of inside information. With the fall of the USSR he became a keen supporter of Yeltsin's policies of free market economics and liberal democracy, later serving as Yeltsin's adviser on defence. These views are reflected in Volkogonov's biography, which presented a highly critical view of Stalin and his policies. Stalin was seen as building on the authoritarianism established under Lenin but going further by his drive for personal power. Stalin had manipulated both the party structures and the largely passive Russian population for his own ends to commit the 'most horrendous crime in the history of Russia'. According to Volkogonov the course of the revolution showed that the only way the Russians would achieve freedom would be through the adoption of liberal democracy. Thus, despite the fall of the USSR and its restrictions on historical study, Russian writers were still finding political dilemmas of the present affecting their view of the past.

Western historiography

Although the general attitude of western historians and commentators has been one of an anti-Stalinist stance, especially during the period of the Cold War after 1945, there has been a variety of approaches. Even during the 1930s the attitude of western commentators was surprisingly mixed.

Western commentators 1930–45. During the 1930s several western journalists were allowed into the Soviet Union and reported what they saw. Walter Duranty's *Russia Reported* (1935) and Eugene Lyons' *Assignment in Utopia* (1937) are both examples of the reflections of American journalists who, as communist sympathisers, were allowed into the USSR. Their first-hand experiences led them to become critical of the Soviet regime, yet it is interesting to note how difficult it was to report accurately. Travel within the Soviet Union was controlled and many foreign journalists had little choice but to repeat the official line of the Soviet government as it was presented through daily news conferences organised by *Tass*, the government's press organisation.

Malcolm Muggeridge, the British commentator, did report on the Ukrainian famine, which was officially denied by the government, after travelling to affected areas. Muggeridge was not believed by other commentators such as the British socialists Sidney and Beatrice Webb, who had also visited the USSR and been taken to collectives by the government; they, however, were showpiece collectives.

Writers from the Left of the political spectrum were keen to see the 'Great Socialist Experiment' in the Soviet Union in a positive light. The economic problems experienced by capitalism in the wake of the Wall Street Crash of 1929 and the growing threat of fascism in Europe seemed to present socialism and the Soviet Union as beneficent alternatives and enabled commentators to overlook more negatives aspects of the Soviet regime. The British government was unwilling to be too critical of the Soviet regime during the 1930s in case they had to establish some sort of relationship with the USSR against Hitler. The Soviet Union might be needed in a future war against Nazi Germany.

The events of the Second World War saw Britain and the USSR on the same side against the fascist powers of Germany and Italy. This alliance continued to shed a positive light on Stalin and the USSR, especially when the Soviet army was able to turn the tide against Germany on the Eastern Front. In the West, the military performance of the USSR commanded respect. The war did have another impact on historical research in the acquisition of the Smolensk Archives. In 1941 the advancing German army captured most of the Communist Party archives in Smolensk. In 1945 they fell into the hands of the American army and were microfilmed before being returned to the Russians. Merle Fainsod used these sources to write an 'uncensored' account of collectivisation. *Smolensk under Russian Rule* (1959) showed the ruthlessness of collectivisation and highlighted how local feuds were sometimes responsible for carrying out local atrocities beyond anything the leadership had intended. The Smolensk Archives gave valuable inside knowledge but related only to a small part of the total area collectivised. It has been suggested that the archives were themselves censored, perhaps twice, once by the Soviet authorities before their capture and secondly by the USA afterwards – both for political purposes.

The Liberal, Intentionalist School after 1945. The period after the end of the Second World War saw the development of the Cold War. This was a time of rapidly declining relations between the USA and the Soviet Union. The hostility generated by the Cold War had an enormous influence on the writing of the history of Stalin's rule in the 1930s.

Shocked by the Soviet Union's lack of freedom and use of terror, historians tried to explain the ruthless policies Stalin had undertaken in the 1930s and which were seen as responsible for the features of the Soviet regime after 1945. Political scientists, particularly in the USA, started to apply the concept of **totalitarianism** to the USSR. This concept focused on a system developed by a leader to gain total control over the economic, social and political life of a nation. This concept was applied to Nazi Germany and Fascist Italy as well as the Soviet Union and in the context of the events of the Second World War and the Cold War that followed, totalitarianism became associated with evil, 'slavery' and lack of freedom.

To the totalitarian school, the origins of this development were important and in the hostility of the Cold War historians in the West were inclined to believe that the evils of totalitarianism were inherent in communism and in the Bolshevik Revolution. Thus Stalin represented a logical extension to the nature of the Bolshevik regime of Lenin.

Also important in the West after 1945 was the intentionalist school. This school of historians can be seen as another product of the values of liberal democracy that have been dominant in the West. They see the role of the individual as of key importance in the process of promoting historical change. Thus, they have centred on the role of Stalin as the motivator behind the policy changes of the 1930s. The policies of Stalin are seen as bearing the stamp of his own personality. In Conquest's *The Harvest of Sorrow* (1986) collectivisation is seen as Stalin's deliberate policy to

KEY CONCEPT

Totalitarianism A concept developed by western historians after 1945 to describe a system whereby a ruler has total control over all aspects of life.

eliminate opposition. In *The Great Terror* (1971) Conquest sees the purges as 'above all Stalin's personal achievement', arguing that 'the one fundamental drive that can be found throughout is his strengthening of his own position'. Bullock (1991) emphasises Stalin's role in the 'Revolution imposed from above' as well as drawing attention to Stalin's paranoid tendencies which stamped his own personality on his policies. To the intentionalist school the role of Stalin was the most important factor in explaining the course of events in the 1930s. They were not merely a continuation of trends established by Lenin.

The Determinist School. In the West, the dominant liberal school of historians was challenged in the 1950s by a more determinist approach adopted by historians who saw the role of Stalin as of less importance. I Deutscher's biography of Stalin (1949) took a Marxist line that socio-economic forces influenced the course of events. Deutscher was a deep but not uncritical admirer of Trotsky and one of the first historians to have access to Trotsky's personal papers. This clearly gave Deutscher's work value. He presented a view of Stalin as a harsh leader but one whose policies were supported and encouraged by a sizeable part of the population.

The British economist A Nove saw Stalinism as a product of the time and circumstances within which Stalin had to operate. His views were put forward in his article *Was Stalinism Necessary?* (1962). The use of force to bring about rapid industrialisation was necessary if a minority group like the Bolsheviks was ever to change a backward economy such as that which existed in the USSR during the 1920s.

E H Carr was another western historian to challenge the tradition that found everything about Stalin repulsive. In *The History of Soviet Russia*, published in the 1950s, Carr steered attention away from Stalin to the institutions of the Soviet State. He concluded that the Bolshevik Revolution would have run into the sand without the changes introduced by Stalin, but that his policies were more a product of the time and the place rather than of Stalin's personality. It should be added that Carr's research was on the years up to 1929, thus he did not go beyond the crucial watershed year; however, his work has been very influential. Revisionist historians since 1980 have picked up on Carr's themes.

The Revisionist School. The 1970s and 1980s saw the emergence of historians challenging the accepted western views of Stalin. Two important approaches within the revisionist school have been those of the structuralists and of social historians. Both approaches have moved attention away from Stalin to examine the 'revolution from below'. The greater availability of sources since *Glasnost* in 1985, especially for the social historian, has given these approaches greater impetus.

Revisionist historians have highlighted the popular support for Stalin's policies. L Viola's *The Best Sons of the Fatherland* (1987) emphasises how the workers who volunteered for the collectivisation brigades saw their work as vital to the survival of the revolution. There was a lot of support in the towns for collectivisation, a point reinforced by C Merrivale in *Moscow Politics and the Rise of Stalin* (1990). R W Davies, in *Industrialisation of Soviet Russia* (1980), highlights the lack of central direction over the collectivisation programme and how the government found it difficult to control local party brigades. A similar pattern has emerged from revisionist studies of industrialisation. Sheila Fitzpatrick's *Cultural Revolution in Russia 1928–31* (1978) highlights the pressure for industrialisation among the workers and party members who were disillusioned with the compromises of the NEP.

Revisionist approaches to the purges have been more controversial. J Arch Getty's *Origins of the Great Purges* (1985) highlights evidence of a plot involving a Trotskyite-Zinoviev bloc. There was, perhaps, evidence to explain the purges other than Stalin's own personal agenda. Social historians have looked at the enormous pressures facing the revolution and how this led to active support for the purging of class enemies, a factor again highlighted by Fitzpatrick. Structuralist historians, such as G Rittersporn in *Stalinist Simplifications and Soviet Complications* (1991), have drawn attention to conflict between the central government and local party authorities, showing the regime as much more chaotic than the totalitarian view of a monolithic state suggested.

Tucker has suggested an approach which combines elements of both the intentionalist and structuralist schools. In his *Stalin in Power* (1990) Tucker highlights how the power of the state interacted with resistance from society to produce a series of advances, such as in 1928–32, followed by periods of consolidation, as in 1933–36, when social opposition led the government to make concessions. This view has been termed the reconstruction-consolidation or 'reccon' approach.

CONCLUSIONS

While not denying that Stalin played a role in the policies of the 1930s, the revisionists have widened the debate by focusing on the involvement of other groups and institutions in policy making. Criticised by the liberal, intentionalist school for rendering Stalin a puppet, the revisionists have, nonetheless, placed Stalin within the wider context of social and economic forces.

It was in response to these circumstances, and the traditions already established by the Bolsheviks under Lenin, that Stalin was able to emerge as leader of the Communist Party and develop his own policies. These policies may have been used to strengthen Stalin's personal power but they were also supported by rank and file party members as measures necessary to ensure the survival of the revolution.

A summary

Lenin and Stalin: change and continuity

Key issue: Did Stalinism mark a turning point in the revolution?

Elements of continuity
- Stalin had few ideas of his own, he merely applied those of Lenin. This was stressed by the Soviet school under Stalin to justify policy decisions.
- The rooting out of class enemies: there is similarity between the aims of Lenin during the civil war (to remove the old order) and those of Stalin under the first Five-Year Plan (aimed at removing Nepmen and kulaks). The policies of the 1930s were driven by attitudes shaped by the civil war under Lenin. This has been emphasised by revisionist historians.
- The party should govern in the interests of the working class. This was the stated aim of both leaders.
- The growth of the bureaucracy: the apparatus of the party and state had grown under Lenin, Stalin merely built on this.
- The use of terror: Lenin had purged political opponents as well as members of his own party. This provided a precedent for Stalin.
- Stalinism grew out of the authoritarian tendencies of Bolshevism which were evident before Stalin. Thus there is continuity with Lenin. The Bolshevik Revolution was therefore the original sin. This view has been stressed by the liberal school who see all aspects of communism in a negative light. Stalin merely highlighted the brutal nature of the Soviet regime. Russian writers since the fall of communism in 1991 have often come to this conclusion.
- Stalin was one of a long line of Russian despotic leaders. Thus the continuity is not just with Lenin but with long-term trends in Russian history which were also responsible for Ivan the Terrible and Peter the Great. This view has been put forward by the 'Russia's Revenge' school in the West which sees Stalin as a 'Red Tsar'.

Elements of change

- Stalin betrayed the revolution by perverting it for his own ends. A Dictatorship of the Proletariat was turned into a personal dictatorship of Stalin. This view was emphasised by Trotsky and his supporters.
- Lenin's use of terror was justified as the civil war threatened the very existence of the regime; Stalin used terror for his own ends.
- Stalin's economic policies marked a break from the NEP. The emphasis was now on coercion rather than compromise. In this sense Stalin broke away from the policies of Lenin. This was emphasised by Soviet writers in the period of *Glasnost*. Supporters of the more conciliatory policies of Bukharin also emphasise this change away from the NEP.
- The revolution was in danger of running into the ground by 1928. The policies of Stalin brought about real changes which saved the revolution. The determinist school emphasises this factor.
- Lenin was tolerant – within limits – of debate within the party; Stalin was intolerant of any dissent.

SECTION 4

How successful was Stalin's attempt to modernise the USSR?

In 1931 Stalin stated that the Soviet Union was 'fifty to one hundred years behind the advanced countries. We must make good this distance in ten years. Either we do it or we shall be crushed'. In 1941 the military might of Nazi Germany invaded the USSR, providing an enormous test for the Soviet Union. The fact that the USSR was able to withstand the attack and ultimately defeat Germany seemed to confirm that Stalin's policies had brought about a successful modernisation of the country. The economic policies of the Five-Year Plans had transformed the Soviet Union from a relatively backward economy into a modern industrial state. Yet the progress made was unbalanced and achieved at an enormous cost.

Heavy industry
Despite problems with the official figures produced by the Soviet government, there is no doubt that the economic achievements of the Five-Year Plans were substantial. Although few industries met the over-ambitious targets of the first Five-Year Plan there was an enormous growth in industrial production.

The historian Nove has drawn attention to some of the issues concerning official production figures, which indicate that production of machinery greatly over-fulfilled the plan despite less success in the production of metal. This appears odd given the obvious connections between the two industries. Nonetheless, there seems to have been rapid growth in the engineering industry and fuel production. Heavy industry in general saw substantial growth. This was due to the focus of the first Five-Year Plan and the concentration of resources it received thereafter.

The first Five-Year Plan increased production by improving efficiency in existing factories as well as developing new industrial plant. The Plans saw the successful completion of projects to provide power for the growth in industry. The Dnieper dam project was one of the most important examples. The Plans developed both traditional industrial centres, such as Moscow and Leningrad, as well as new centres in the less developed parts of the country. Both Kazakhstan and Georgia saw significant industrial development. The success of the second Five-Year Plan owed a lot to the fact that new industrial centres started under the first Plan were now completed and in production. The coal and steel industries expanded

**The Dnieper
Dam Project.**

rapidly in the early 1930s. The period 1928 to 1941 saw a fourfold
increase in steel and a six fold increase in coal production. And this was at
a time when the rest of the world was suffering economic decline due to
the impact of the Great Depression. Thus although targets were not met,
in many cases the achievement was still very impressive.

Chaotic implementation and planning have often been highlighted as
factors which limited the economic achievements of economic policy.
The state's rigid adoption of a command economy, directed by the
government, led to failures because planners based in Moscow had little
understanding of local conditions in the far-flung parts of the Soviet
Union. The result was that many resources were wasted because they were
inappropriate. The imposition of over-ambitious production targets by
central government on factories throughout the country encouraged local
managers to be creative. This included hijacking trains full of workers and
other resources and diverting them to different factories. Creativity with
production figures led to corruption which later became an integral part
of the Soviet economy. Interference by the party was a significant factor
in 1937, when the disruption caused by the removal of many managers
during the purges led to an economic slowdown.

Consumer industry

The enormous improvements made in heavy industry were not matched by progress in consumer industry. Textile production actually declined under the first Five-Year Plan. This was largely due to the collapse in livestock numbers caused by the introduction of collectivisation. The second and third Plans attempted to increase consumer goods but with the increase in international tension, resources were redirected back towards heavy industry and armaments. Despite this there was some advance in consumer goods. Footwear production and food processing made significant increases. By the late 1930s these developments were starting to have some impact on living standards. New bakeries, ice-cream and meat-packing factories were established in many towns. These improvements, although welcome, did not solve the problem of shortages of important consumer goods.

Labour conditions

If substantial economic progress was achieved it was on the back of extremely harsh working conditions. The Plans called for workers to devote all their energies to achieving the targets set under each Plan. The first Five-Year Plan had to rely on revolutionary fervour to motivate a workforce that was largely unskilled. In 1933 only 17 per cent of the workforce in Moscow were skilled. Training schemes were introduced that started to transform the workforce. The percentage of unskilled workers in industry dropped considerably through the 1930s, although problems continued in some areas. The government increased the wages of trained and skilled workers in order to encourage workers to acquire the skills necessary to improve productivity. Revolutionary fervour still played its part through the Stakhanovite movement. These shock-brigades of Communist Party members were designed to instil the workforce with socialist values in order to promote production.

The high level of absenteeism was evidence that not all workers were convinced by the slogans of the party. Work discipline was improved by the introduction of harsh penalties for slackers. In the last resort, the government could always use slave labour to complete large building projects, as it did for the White Sea Canal. The conditions endured by slave labour meant that many died before the task was completed. This seems to illustrate the attitude of Stalin and his government that the cost was of no consequence providing the task was accomplished.

Agriculture

The human cost of collectivisation was enormous. The elimination of fifteen million kulaks represents a human tragedy of epic proportions. In addition to this there were an estimated four million deaths from the famine in 1933 despite official statements by the Soviet government denying its existence. The historian Robert Conquest (1986) has argued that collectivisation, with its resulting famine, was a deliberate policy of genocide against the Ukrainian people on the part of Stalin. An analysis of the grain harvest in 1932 indicates it was low in most areas of the Soviet Union, but as the chief grain-growing region of the country, the Ukraine bore the brunt of this food shortage. The case of the Kazakhs illustrates another side to the human cost. This nomadic group was forced into collectives against their will. The change in their way of life had devastating consequences. Their sheep flocks were virtually wiped out and a typhus epidemic reduced the Kazakh population by 40 per cent.

In economic terms the results of collectivisation were devastating: there was a disastrous decline in cattle from over 70 million in 1928 to less than 39 million in 1933; grain production fell from 73.3 million tonnes in 1928 to 67.7 million tonnes in 1934. Although the more widespread use of agricultural machinery led to some recovery in the late 1930s, productivity levels remained extremely low. It took decades for Soviet agriculture to reach some of the production figures for foodstuffs attained in the period before collectivisation.

Urbanisation

The industrialisation of the Soviet Union brought about a swift increase in urbanisation. This rapid change was an important element in the modernisation of the Soviet Union. Long-established cities grew with the move of population from the countryside into towns. Moscow's population increased from 2.2 million in 1929 to 3.6 million in 1936. Leningrad saw even greater growth, from 1.6 million in 1926 to 3.5 million in 1939. Many new cities also emerged from the industrial development of the 1930s. The towns of the Donbass coal and steel region saw a doubling of their population in the 1930s. The historian Moshe Lewin (1975) has challenged the view that this development constitutes rapid urbanisation. He argues that because towns and cities were swamped by people from rural areas, bringing their rural attitudes and values with them, the term 'ruralisation' is a better description for this process than urbanisation. The development of new industrial centres, such as Magnitogorsk, certainly lacked the range of facilities usually associated with towns and cities. In the rush to industrialise, resources for housing and entertainment were often non-existent. Workers had to sleep in tents, makeshift huts or even in the factories.

Living standards

Judging the standard of living in any country at any time is a difficult process. As a concept it involves far more than wages compared with prices: it includes such aspects as housing, services, social security and how these relate to the values of society in terms of its expectations. To consider the concept as it applies to a country such as the USSR based on socialist values is even more difficult.

Nove (1969) has described the early years of the first Five-Year Plan as bringing about 'the most precipitous decline in living standards known in recorded history'. He uses the neglect of consumer goods, food shortages, rationing and poor quality of goods as evidence. Although conditions improved after 1933, real wages stayed below the figure for 1928.

By 1935 the rationing of meat and bread had ended and all rationing was abolished in 1936. Cheap food was available within the workforce canteens and work clothes were given free of charge. Public transport was developed, especially in the large towns and cities, but trams remained grossly overcrowded. Unemployment was not a problem given the shortage of labour caused by industrialisation, but much of the work was hard, repetitive and mentally unchallenging. Living conditions remained far below those illustrated in official propaganda with its images of modern city life, but improvements were in evidence. The allocation of a modern apartment with running water, electricity and central heating was a realistic hope for those workers who showed an impressive commitment to fulfilling the plan. For the rest of the population, housing remained drab and overcrowded and conditions in the countryside remained primitive compared with those in towns.

Social transformation

An important aspect of modernisation under the Five-Year Plans was the transformation of society. The removal of 'bourgeois' capitalist elements, the kulaks and Nepmen, who were seen as holding back the development of a modern socialist society, was an integral part of the policies pursued in the 1930s. The process of collectivisation removed the village priest and traditional school teacher as well as the kulaks. State control over the economy removed the Nepmen, private traders and owners of small businesses who had profited under the NEP. This was a war waged against the enemies of socialism within the Soviet Union, and the government presented the implementation of the Five-Year Plans in militaristic terms.

In 1936 Stalin stated that only three classes now existed in Soviet society: the working class, the peasantry and the 'working intelligentsia' (this included administrators and managers). In terms of moving towards a socialist utopia, society had been transformed.

The 1930s had seen the Soviet Union change rapidly from a relatively backward agricultural-based economy into a modern industrial-based economy and this was reflected in the resulting social change. It was an impressive transformation both in terms of economic achievement and in its speed. Yet the improvements were not felt in all aspects of the economy, with consumer industry and agriculture lagging behind. The 1930s had seen a battle for resources between industry and agriculture, which had led to a victory for the former at the expense of the latter. The resulting division would remain deep and lasting. The human cost of the economic development of the Soviet Union would also leave deep wounds, and the issue of whether the economic achievements were worth the cost has been a source of debate among historians.

WAS STALINISM NECESSARY?

In their assessments of Stalin's economic policies, historians have weighed up the achievements against the cost. This issue has been tied to a consideration of whether Stalin's policies were necessary. Were there alternative methods of achieving the aims of the Communist Party? This has led to a range of differing viewpoints, which are often based on the philosophical standpoint of the writer.

The Liberal School

Works by western commentators during the 1930s tended to see Stalin's reforms in a positive light. Commentators with communist sympathies were allowed to visit the Soviet Union and their subsequent reports about the 'Great Socialist Experiment' were generally positive. These views were reinforced by comparisons with the fascist states of Nazi Germany and Mussolini's Italy. Those commentators, such as Malcolm Muggeridge, who reported on negative aspects like the Ukrainian famine, were either not believed or overlooked, as the British government tried to foster better relations with the USSR as an ally against fascism in the 1930s. When the Second World War was over and the Cold War developed, relations between the West and the USSR became more hostile and the views of historians in the West reflected this.

Not surprisingly, the liberal school of historians, which developed in the West after the Second World War, has been highly critical of the cost of Stalin's achievements. Although there has been some acknowledgement of economic progress made in the 1930s, historians of the liberal school have seen the human cost as too great to justify what was achieved. Historians such as Robert Conquest in *Harvest of Sorrow* (1986) have drawn attention to the enormous human cost of Stalin's programme of collectivisation. The horrors of the work camps and the harsh conditions industrial workers were forced to endure during the Five-Year Plans have also been highlighted.

The approach of this school has been influenced by the values of liberal democracy in the West, that see individual and economic freedom as important. From this standpoint Stalin's policies of state control supported by widespread use of terror and fear cannot be justified. It has highlighted the evils, and the lack of freedom associated with totalitarian regimes.

The Determinist School

There have been challenges to the dominant liberal school in the West since the 1950s. Some historians have taken the view that Stalin and his policies were a product of their time and circumstances. In this sense they were determined by the context within which they operated. Historians taking this approach have tried to present a balanced picture of Stalin. A Nove, the British economist, saw Stalinism as an economically unavoidable outcome of an insecure government, desperate to industrialise in the face of impending attack. In his article *Was Stalin really necessary?* (1962) Nove concluded that the circumstances made Stalinism necessary. Given the USSR's economic backwardness and the fact that the Bolsheviks were a minority group, they could achieve rapid industrialisation only if force was used. Thus Stalinism was necessary, even if not desirable. Although recognising the human cost, Nove saw Stalinism as effective, and was one of the first historians in the West to highlight some of its strengths.

Revisionist historians

The views of the liberal school have been challenged further by the revisionist school of historians which has developed since the 1980s. Making use of the sources available since the collapse of the USSR, social historians have been able to examine the process of modernisation at local level in more depth than was previously possible. Studies by Sheila Fitzpatrick, R W Davies and L Viola have all found evidence of the pressures to modernise from the rank and file of the Communist Party. Their research indicates a high level of disillusionment with the compromises of the NEP. Thus the forced industrialisation of the Five-Year Plans was supported by sections of the population; a view that seems to challenge the notion that economic policy was merely an instrument of Stalin's dictatorship.

Soviet historiography

The Soviet view under Stalin (1928–53). The control of the Soviet government over the press and other publications severely restricted the debate within the Soviet Union. The role of official publications was to support the policies of Stalin as necessary measures to safeguard the revolution from within and from abroad. The *Short Course* of 1938 presented this view of Stalin's economic policies and became the standard work for other writers who wished to survive.

Trotsky and other émigrés. Uncensored assessments of Stalin's policies by Communist Party members were restricted to the writings of émigrés, those who had fled the USSR. The most important of these was Trotsky. Trotsky's criticisms were centred on the growth of a huge bureaucracy that betrayed the revolution by using it for its own ends. He saw Stalin as representing this trend. In terms of criticising Stalin's economic policies,

Trotsky was less convincing. He had strongly supported the ending of the NEP during the 1920s and had advocated the forced collectivisation and rapid industrialisation which Stalin undertook during the Five-Year Plans. There is no reason to expect that the economic policies undertaken by Trotsky would have been very different.

Bukharin, on the other hand, was a reminder that there were possible alternatives to the rapid industrialisation of the Five-Year Plans. He had advocated keeping the NEP. His supporters point to the economic progress made under the NEP in 1926 and believed that there was the potential for continued progress. As Bukharin had stated during the dispute over the NEP in the late 1920s, forcible collectivisation would lower productivity among the peasants and slow down the pace of industrialisation. Yet opponents of the NEP argued that the peasants were already slowing the pace of industrialisation and that this was unacceptable. They described this situation as 'riding towards socialism on a peasant nag'.

Bukharin's interviews with the Menshevik historian Boris Nicolaevsky in 1936 presented the view of Stalin using policies, not for modernising the Soviet Union, but as instruments to establish a personal dictatorship. Bukharin was, of course, a bitter man by this time and this bitterness is reflected in his views. He did, however, have first-hand experience of Stalin's methods.

Soviet historiography from Khrushchev to Gorbachev (1953–85). After the death of Stalin in 1953 there was a reassessment of Stalin's work in the Soviet Union. Caught up in the process of destalinisation, introduced by Khrushchev, official Soviet historical writing adopted a more critical view of Stalin's policies. The new official *History of the Communist Party*, published in 1959, accused Stalin of economic mistakes and 'errors'. Khrushchev's own statements also made heavy criticisms of the use of terror. Although these 'mistakes' and 'errors' were condemned, the general thrust of Stalin's economic policies was not challenged.

Under the leadership of Brezhnev (1964–82) Soviet writers tended to ignore the role of Stalin rather than offer direct criticism. Although this view, which seemed to underplay the importance of individuals in the process of historical change, followed a traditional Marxist line, it was also prompted by political considerations. Brezhnev did not want to extend destalinisation and feared criticism of elements of Stalinism would promote further destalinisation.

Not all Soviet writers during this period rigidly followed the official government line. Roy Medvedev, a dissident who was critical of the regime, rejected the idea that Stalinism was inevitable. In *Let History*

Judge (1971) he acknowledged the economic achievements of Stalin's policies but he also emphasised the cost, which he described as a 'black shadow' cast over the period.

After 1985, when Gorbachev's policy of *Glasnost* (openness) encouraged free debate and criticism of the Soviet past, there was a re-examination of the alternatives to Stalinism. Attention was focused on the ideas of Bukharin and the NEP. The mix of private and state-controlled industry within the economy was very much in tune with the economic restructuring attempted by Gorbachev in the second half of the 1980s. Gorbachev argued that the NEP could have delivered the modernisation of the Soviet Union that was required in the 1930s, just as it could rejuvenate the Soviet economy in the 1980s.

Russian writers since 1991. The openness which followed from *Glasnost* led to more fundamental criticisms of the role of Communism. Russian writers questioned the whole communist experience, not just Stalinism. Dmitri Volkogonov (1990) was highly critical of Stalin. He argued that the only way to modernise Russia in the fullest sense of the word was to adopt liberal democracy as in the West. It should be noted that Volkogonov's viewpoint was a reflection of both his own past experiences living under the Soviet regime and his position as an adviser to Boris Yeltsin, the Russian President who aimed to move the country towards free market economics and liberal democracy during the 1990s. This view has similarities with those of the liberal school in the West.

CONCLUSION

At the end of the 1990s there was the start of a growing consensus among many historians that the economic policies pursued by Stalin to modernise the Soviet Union were unnecessary. Both the liberal school in the West and Russian writers since 1991 have emphasised the enormous human cost of the policies and Stalin's personal manipulation of policy to his own advantage. They also see the existence of valid alternatives. Yet just when there has been growing support for these views, they have been challenged by revisionist historians. To see the economic policies of the 1930s as merely instruments of Stalin's personal power would be very misleading. Stalin and his supporters defended the Five-Year Plans and collectivisation as necessary tools in the process of strengthening the revolution to ensure its survival. These were measures which had the active encouragement of rank and file party members.

SECTION 5

Propaganda and the cult of personality – how popular was Stalin?

Any support for Stalin was, according to the traditional view of western historians, imposed through the Soviet regime's excessive use of propaganda. In the light of the considerable hardships endured by the population during the Five-Year Plans and the use of terror through the purges, popular support for Stalin was seen as manufactured by the government rather than real and active support. The development of the cult of personality around Stalin was seen as a symbol of the development of this manufactured support. Research undertaken by revisionist historians has challenged this viewpoint, seeing the government responding to public opinion as well as attempting to mobilise it from above.

BY WHAT METHODS, AND WITH WHAT SUCCESS, DID THE SOVIET REGIME USE PROPAGANDA TO MOBILISE SUPPORT FOR ITS POLICIES?

The Soviet government had a wide range of means of attempting to mobilise public opinion in its favour. Propaganda designed to influence the views and attitudes of the Soviet population could be conveyed through a range of strategies. The purpose of this propaganda was to reinforce a belief in the achievements of socialism and of the Soviet government. These were not always the same. The development of a cult of personality was an indication that propaganda was being used as an instrument of the leadership rather than of the needs of socialism. The cult of personality was only one of the methods used to mobilise support for the regime. State-controlled youth organisations; education; the media; the arts and popular culture; political rituals; and leisure activities all provided the government with ways of distributing propaganda to get their message across.

Methods:

The cult of personality. The Soviet government developed two cults of personality in the 1920s and 1930s. As soon as Lenin was buried, he was hailed as the hero of the revolution. Images of Lenin appeared in many forms: in newspapers, statues and the cinema. His likeness was used to motivate the population to imitate his commitment to the revolution. The embalming of Lenin for display in the mausoleum in Red Square, in the centre of Moscow, was the most striking example of this use of Lenin as a focus for political purposes. Petrograd was renamed Leningrad in 1924 in honour of his achievements for the revolution. There is no doubt that there was a wave of support for Lenin at the time of his death and the Soviet government was able to build on this. The long queues to see the embalmed body of Lenin were evidence of this support. For Stalin, who actively promoted himself as the worthy continuer of the work of Lenin, this cult was very useful politically.

The second cult of personality that developed was that of Stalin himself. As early as 1923 the town of Tsaritsyn was renamed Stalingrad. Soon after Lenin's death in 1924, the slogan 'Stalin is the Lenin of today' became widely used by sections of the rank and file party members. In the 1930s Stalin was seen by sections of the party as the saviour of socialism against the capitalist elements who were ready to undermine the revolution. This popularity was built up through propaganda, which presented endless images of Stalin as a great leader. Stalin was 'the big hero' or *Vozhd* (the boss). Propaganda posters also highlighted Stalin as a man of the people with images of Stalin and worker, Stalin and peasant and so on. These were ironic images given that Stalin rarely met the average Soviet citizen after 1930. Yet Stalin was always presented as a down-to-earth man happy in his rather plain clothes and smoking a pipe.

The cult of personality centred on Stalin became more evident at the end of the 1930s. There was a lot of advantage to be gained in using one person as a focus for loyalty at a time of impending war. The cult of personality made use of traditional Russian attitudes; the population had been used to expressing their loyalty to the country through one person during the rule of the tsars. The glorification of the state through its leader was a familiar Russian characteristic. After the Second World War this cult of personality rose to ridiculous heights. By 1953 many towns had been renamed after Stalin. The Volga-Don Canal may have carried little traffic but it was littered with statues of Stalin along its banks.

Youth organisations and education. The Soviet government recognised the importance of targeting the attitudes of the young. The main vehicles used in this respect were the youth organisations of the Communist Party and the education system. Party youth organisations consisted of the Pioneers for those under 14 and Komsomol for ages 14 to 28. Komsomol played a central role in the Cultural Revolution of the early 1930s. It was used by the government to attack elements of 'bourgeois' culture and class enemies. This form of mobilisation was in many cases too successful as the government had difficulty keeping control over the movement and it had to intervene to bring an end to its excesses. The example of Pavlik Morozov illustrates the power behind the mobilisation of youth. Morozov was a fourteen-year-old from the Urals who became famous in the early

The image of Stalin lights up the Moscow skies.

1930s for denouncing his own father to the authorities. His father was accused of association with the kulaks. Morozov was used by the government in a campaign to encourage young people to inform on anyone suspected of 'bourgeois tendencies'. When Morozov was murdered by members of his own family, the government treated him as a martyr and erected statues in his honour.

The success of Komsomol was reflected in the membership figures. In 1929 there were 2.3 million members, rising to 10.2 million in 1940. These members provided a valuable reservoir of labour motivated by revolutionary fervour that could be used on major building projects. Many Komsomol members volunteered to go to Magnitogorsk to build the new city.

The attitudes of the young were easier to influence than those of the older generation and the government recognised the importance of education in bringing about change. The Cultural Revolution had been useful in removing teachers who were not committed to socialism but the chaos that followed was unlikely to produce the moulding of attitudes the government desired. The Education Law of 1935 reasserted discipline in schools and government direction over the curriculum. The prescription of textbooks by the government ensured propaganda in support of the government was conveyed. The *Short Course* became a standard text. As a history of the Communist Party it presented the Stalinist view. It is probable that Stalin himself wrote the chapter on 'Dialectical and Historical Materialism'.

The media. Government control over newspapers and the radio ensured that the Soviet population received a very narrow range of views. *Pravda* and *Izvestiya*, the two leading newspapers, were used for propaganda, highlighting the achievements of the Five-Year Plans. Access to printing presses was restricted to those whose interests did not conflict with 'the interests of the workers and the Socialist order'. This term was, of course, defined by the government. Radio stations were controlled by the government and conveyed the official message alongside light or classical music. The limits on the amount of information given to the population were important in restricting the level of public debate.

The arts and popular culture. The focus on accessible art and popular culture provided a useful propaganda instrument. All forms of art and popular culture were controlled by the government. Writers and artists were expected to work within limits laid down by the government.

The Soviet authorities attacked 'high culture' as elitist and 'bourgeois'. For propaganda purposes 'high culture' was of limited use if few of the population could understand its meaning. The emphasis on the cult of the 'little man', in the early 1930s, was an attempt to make the arts more relevant to the hopes and desires of the industrial workforce. Soviet agencies, such as RAPP, did their best to encourage cultural activities in the workplace.

The return to more traditional cultural values after 1932 gave the government more success in tapping into themes that were popular. In writing, the emphasis on heroes connected to the party built on the traditions of Russian folk heroes. Socialist Realism, rooted in 'the people', resulted in formalised but accessible styles in art and writing. The images presented were propaganda: idealised images of life in the Soviet Union. It is easy to criticise Socialist Realism for being so out of touch with reality but the work of social historians such as R Stites, has drawn attention to the range of purposes that the arts and culture could have. Socialist Realism presented images that some committed party members were willing to believe and that others were prepared to use in order to inspire them to work harder; other sections of the population, while not believing them, may have found the images to be a satisfying method of escapism.

There was a lighter mood in the arts and popular culture after 1932, which seemed to coincide with the people's wish to celebrate the successes of the first Five-Year Plan. This mood was checked again in 1936 when the government wished to promote a more solemn and dignified stance. Jazz music suffered; accused of promoting homosexuality, drugs and promiscuity, it faced renewed restrictions. The government's constant changing of emphasis in popular culture was, according to the historian R Stites, a reflection of 'the leadership's desire to capture mass audiences and to respond to the new taste culture generated by the Stalinist social revolution'. What made this possible was the emphasis on mass culture which could be understood by all. The low prices for books and theatre seats also helped to give people access to popular culture.

It is too easy to sneer at the mediocrity of much of the official Soviet culture but the developments of the 1930s did lead to an increased appetite among workers and peasants for cultural activities. The rise in education standards for the general population and the growth in the number of party officials generated a wide range of cultural tastes which government policy alone could not meet.

Government manipulation and control of the arts and popular culture was able to work at different levels. It served a range of functions: it was a source of information; it provided entertainment; it was a useful form of escapism; and it offered opportunities for socialising. It was rather more than art for art's sake. This range of functions gave the government many opportunities to use the arts and popular culture to mobilise support for the regime at a range of levels.

Discussions of political issues and political rituals. The government used carefully controlled public debate as a mechanism for mobilising the people and encouraging mass participation. Discussion of the Soviet Constitution of 1936 and the ban on abortions were examples of the use of this strategy. Election campaigns provided other opportunities to discuss and debate policies within the strict framework laid down by the party.

The Stakhanovite movement can be seen in part as an instrument of the government in building on the hopes of some workers who wanted to improve their status and rewards. The use of words such as 'wrecker' and 'saboteur' by government leaders was picked up by industrial workers who looked for reasons to explain why they were unable to meet the achievements set by Stakhanov. The factory managers were targeted as easy scapegoats for the lack of available resources.

Even more sinister was the government's use of show trials during the Great Terror. They were used by the government as political rituals, which mobilised sectors of the population against the class enemy within the Soviet Union.

Leisure and public celebrations. The Soviet government made use of public celebrations to mobilise the population. The celebration of the Pushkin centennial of 1937 was particularly effective. Celebrations of the anniversary of the October Revolution became large government-managed events. There were other achievements that could be used by the government as a source of pride in the Soviet state, such as the achievements of the Five-Year Plans, and public events were used to celebrate them. Successful expeditions to the Arctic and northern Russia in search of gold and oil were part of a theme which struck a chord with many Soviet citizens: the triumph of technology over nature. The aviators who flew over the North Pole were greeted by Stalin as conquering heroes. They represented bravery, adventure and the pushing back of frontiers.

All organised leisure was run by the state. Sport facilities became widespread in the late 1930s and leisure activities were to develop into important means of mobilising the population. Football became a mass spectator sport and Moscow's two leading teams, Dynamo and Spartak, developed large followings. Exhibitions were very popular. Moscow's Agricultural Exhibition of 1939 attracted 30,000 people every day. Gorky Park, in Moscow, received hundreds of thousands of visitors at the weekend. The park included a swimming pool, dance area and a theatre, with seating for 25,000 people. By 1940 there were over 28,000 cinemas in the Soviet Union.

Assessment of results

The Cultural Revolution and the Great Terror removed nearly all other forms of association outside the state and allowed the government a high level of control as the sole provider of information. The horrors of collectivisation, the great famine and the terror played little part in the popular culture of the 1930s. The government was able to spread propaganda through many vehicles to focus minds on more uplifting themes. 'Life has become more joyous', exclaimed Stalin in 1935, and popular songs developed this theme. It was a useful form of escapism.

Not all sectors of the population were willing to go along with the government line. There were sections of the rural population that remained hostile to the regime. The horrors endured in the name of collectivisation had left a deep and lasting hatred for the Soviet government in some parts of the countryside.

Despite government controls, sub-cultures and counter-cultures continued. The wide variety of popular culture provided the government with an impossible task in its attempts to control all aspects of culture.

Mobilising the people: a women's march in Moscow.

The return to traditional folk culture at the end of the 1930s was, in part, a recognition of this. The counter-culture of the outcasts from Stalinist society was an unintentional result of Stalin's policies. The gulag and the underground groups of orphans and street gangs developed their own culture of jokes, songs, slang and even worshipped their own martyrs.

Conclusions

The view, common in the West during the period of the Cold War, that the Soviet population was cowed by terror and force is too simplistic. Terror and force were important methods of social control but the Soviet government was able to use a wide range of strategies to mobilise the population's support. Propaganda was at its most successful when it built on trends and themes that already existed in Soviet society. Yet it could work at different levels in order to maximise its chances of having an impact on attitudes and behaviour. Stalin's task was made easier by the relative naivety of a population caught up in rapid economic and social change.

HOW POPULAR WERE STALIN AND HIS POLICIES?

Historians have often portrayed the USSR as a totalitarian regime which used terror and propaganda as instruments of mobilising the people. The traditional view of Stalin's policies was that they were imposed on a largely unwilling population cowed into submission by terror and fear. Since the fall of the Soviet Union there has been a greater availability of sources and this has allowed social historians to challenge this view. They have examined developments from 'below' as part of the general challenging of the liberal intentionalist approach which focuses on the government leadership. This has revealed a surprising level of support for Stalin and his policies among the Soviet population.

Soviet historiography

Soviet historiography during the period of Stalin's leadership emphasised the important role of Stalin in directing the revolution and presented him as a genius adored by a grateful people. The official biography of Stalin by G F Alexandrov (1949) is a good example of the hagiography churned out by the government in this period. Yet Soviet historiography poses particular problems for the student of history because the very process of writing history in the Soviet Union was itself part of the official Soviet culture.

It is hardly surprising, therefore, that Soviet historians saw Stalin's achievements in a positive light. Stalin's policies were seen as necessary measures to safeguard the revolution. The emphasis on the importance of

Stalin was part of the development of a cult of personality and it was this aspect which was criticised after Stalin's death.

After 1953, Khrushchev's policies encouraged some criticism of aspects of Stalinism. Khrushchev attacked the cult of personality as 'the elevation of one person, his transformation into a superman possessing supernatural characteristics, akin to those of a god... Such a belief about Stalin was cultivated among us for many years'. This criticism of Stalin was itself part of the political process of destalinisation undertaken by Khrushchev.

It was not until 1985, when the new Soviet leader Gorbachev encouraged *Glasnost* (openness), that a greater degree of genuine freedom resulted in a more critical approach to Stalin. This process brought about a virtually wholesale rubbishing of Stalin and his policies. The use of terror against the Soviet population was highlighted as evidence of Stalinism being imposed from above. Russian writers since 1991, such as Dmitri Volkogonov, have tended to reflect this trend of distancing the Soviet past from the present. This approach is partly connected with the needs of a Russian population still trying to come to terms with its Stalinist past. It is comforting to be able to blame the horrors of Stalin's policies on one person and there is, perhaps, an element of looking for an easy scapegoat to blame for the evils of the 1930s.

The Liberal School

The liberal school of historians in the West has tended to take a negative view of Stalinism. This viewpoint was reinforced by émigrés from the aristocracy who left Russia during the revolution. Thus it was an approach rooted in the experiences and preferences of those who were against the revolution and who saw liberal democracy in the West as a better guarantee of freedom of expression.

The hostility generated by the Cold War had an enormous influence on the writing of the history of Stalin's rule in the 1930s. Shocked by the Soviet Union's lack of freedom and use of terror, historians tried to explain the ruthless policies Stalin had undertaken in the 1930s and which were seen as responsible for the features of the Soviet regime after 1945. Political scientists, particularly in the USA, started to apply the concept of totalitarianism to the USSR. This concept focused on a system developed by a leader to gain total control over the economic, social and political life of a nation. It involved:

- state control of the entire economy
- the mobilisation of the population by the state to rid the country of enemies
- state control over all forms of communication
- the large-scale use of terror to supervise the population

- adulation of a single leader
- the imposition of a single ideology.

Using these methods the position of the leader could be secured through the creation of a monolithic system (acting as one solid block) with every aspect of life centrally controlled. This system was applied to Nazi Germany and Fascist Italy as well as to the Soviet Union. Important works have included H Arendt's *The Origins of Totalitarianism* (1973) and L Schapiro's *Totalitarianism* (1972). In relation to the events of the Second World War and the Cold War which followed, totalitarianism became associated with evil, lack of freedom and 'slavery'. The terminology of totalitarianism was used by many as an insult and in the process it became a less meaningful term.

What the totalitarian approach achieved was to highlight the differences between liberal democracy, the dominant political system in the West, and the Soviet Union. This drew attention to what were seen as the negative attributes of the Soviet system, a useful exercise in itself when the USSR was seen as trying to fulfil the aim of world revolution by expansionist policies during the Cold War. This was a view of history put forward by those influenced by the values of liberalism.

The totalitarian approach saw Stalin and the leadership in control of all aspects of policy, with society weak and at the mercy of decisions imposed by the leadership. As society was inundated with officially approved culture and all independent sources of information were removed, the population had little choice but to accept what the government told them.

The totalitarian approach was reinforced by the type of sources utilised: official decrees, accounts of Westerners who had visited the USSR and the memoirs of émigrés. The majority of personal accounts and memoirs were heavily biased against the regime and, as East-West relations deteriorated during the Cold War, they seemed to confirm the West's suspicions about the nature of communism.

Despite its limitations the totalitarian approach remains valuable in drawing attention to the methods used by the leadership to mobilise support from above. The level of control could not fail to influence people's values and attitudes as V Bonnell showed in 'The Representation of Politics and the Politics of Representation' (*Russian Review*, 1988).

Although totalitarianism has become a less popular term for historians to use, the underlying principles of the liberal school – of power imposed by a leadership against the will of the people – have continued through the intentionalist school. This school of historians sees the role of the individual as of key importance in the process of promoting historical change. Thus, they have centred on the role of Stalin as the motivator behind the policy changes of the 1930s. Because intentionalists focus on the leader, this approach is usually found in biographies. Although dominant in the Cold War period, this school still has its supporters, including Conquest and Bullock.

The Revisionist School

Although the range of sources available to the historian of social and cultural history was very narrow until the 1980s, there were early challenges to the liberal school. It has only been since *Glasnost* and the collapse of the USSR in 1991 that accessibility to sources has been much wider, allowing the assumptions of the totalitarian and intentionalist approaches to be more effectively challenged.

By studying the values, attitudes and actions of groups within Soviet society during the 1930s, revisionist historians have found a degree of popular support for Stalin and his policies that challenges the assumptions made by the totalitarian school of historians. An important aspect of revisionist studies has been to challenge the totalitarian assumption of the power of the leadership to shape and control policy. Social historians have examined the role of social groups in influencing decision-making. They have also been able to consider the range of methods the government could use to mobilise support. This has moved the debate on from rather simplistic notions about the use of terror and propaganda. Structuralist approaches have examined the structures and organisations within the Communist Party to highlight the interaction between local and central government bodies.

To the revisionists the government was often acting from a position of weakness. They stress the hesitation on the part of the leadership and question the assumption that official statements were obeyed. This trend has been highlighted in connection with a wide range of policy:

- G Rittersporn in *Stalinist Simplifications and Soviet Complications* (1991) drew attention to the pressures within the lower ranks of the Communist Party that played an important part in the purges.
- L Viola in *The Best Sons of the Fatherland* (1987) and R W Davies in *Industrialisation of Soviet Russia* (1980), have shown that there was genuine enthusiasm for Stalin's economic policies among party members.
- Sheila Fitzpatrick in *Cultural Revolution in Russia* (1978) put forward the notion of a 'Cultural Revolution' stemming from pressures generated not by the leadership but by disillusioned rank and file party members and Komsomol enthusiasts who wished to eliminate

'bourgeois' elements and create a new society. In this context the leadership was reacting to social forces.

- Fitzpatrick (1994) highlights the importance of attitudes among the rank and file party membership in actively supporting the regime. Their desire for the status, privileges and authority associated with promotion within the party led to a keenness to show their commitment to the revolutionary cause. It was these groups within the party that provided it with a solid base of support. R Service (1997) has also drawn attention to this: 'A new social class was in the process of formation'.
- V Dunham's *In Stalin's Time: Middleclass Values in Soviet Fiction* (1976) shows cultural life under Stalin to be more complex than the totalitarian approach suggests. R Stites (1992) draws attention to the wide variety within Soviet popular culture, indicating that it could not all be controlled by the government.

The value of much of the revisionist work has been its challenging of traditional assumptions about the degree of support for Stalin and his policies. Revisionist approaches have been criticised by intentionalist historians for rendering Stalin a puppet of wider social forces. The keenness to use newly available sources concerned with social history has, perhaps, allowed attention to drift too far away from the role of the leadership. While not denying the power of Stalin to impose decisions, it is now clear that the situation, as it related to the general population, was more complex than the totalitarian approach had shown. One indication of the degree of support Stalin's policies enjoyed has come from A Inkeles and R M Bauer in *The Soviet Citizen* (1959). Interviews with Soviet citizens who fled the country showed support for the welfare policies, the strong government, and a sense of national pride. And this was from those who had left the country!

HEINEMANN ADVANCED HISTORY

SECTION 6

The Stalinist State after 1941

THE IMPACT OF THE SECOND WORLD WAR ON THE SOVIET UNION 1941–45

The German invasion of the Soviet Union in 1941 was the start of a bitter and ferocious struggle. It lasted four years and placed an almost unbearable strain on the Soviet people. The losses, both civilian and military, endured by the USSR were of a scale unknown in modern times. The weaknesses revealed by the initial attack in 1941 were overcome and with an enormous effort on the part of the Soviet population the regime survived this struggle to defeat the might of Hitler's Germany. It was a conflict which revealed both the strengths and weaknesses of the Stalinist regime.

When the Germans invaded at dawn on 22 June 1941 the Soviet Union's initial response showed the weaknesses of a rigid system of government. Stalin was so shocked by the invasion that he seems to have suffered a breakdown. He retired to his dacha for several days, leaving communication with the front confused, until coaxed into action by Molotov. By the end of 1941 the Germans had captured the Baltic States, Belorussia, and the Ukraine, laid siege to Leningrad and reached the outskirts of Moscow. In the face of such losses the Soviet regime had to adapt quickly to the demands of the war in order to survive.

The centralisation of the economy, which was an integral feature of the Stalinist system, proved to be effective in mobilising the resources of the Soviet Union for war. It was a mammoth task. Sixteen per cent of the Soviet population was drafted into the armed forces, providing them with over eleven million people under arms. Production had to be geared to the demands of the war effort.

The economy showed itself capable of improvising to the needs of war. At local level Defence Committees were set up to co-ordinate war production. Despite the collapse in industrial output, which occurred in the immediate aftermath of the invasion, Soviet industrial production rose impressively after 1941. The most able-bodied men from the collectives were conscripted into the armed forces and women provided the bulk of the agricultural workforce. Grain output fell from 95 million tonnes in 1940 to 30 million tonnes in 1942 and the number of cattle halved. In these circumstances the government lifted restrictions on the cultivation of private plots to provide an incentive for peasants to keep up production.

The co-ordination of the country's administration during the war proved the regime's ability to integrate civilian and military aspects of government to the advantage of the war effort. To direct the war effort the State Defence Committee (GKO) was set up. The military were coordinated through the Supreme Command (*Stavka*). It was an administrative system, which worked well for the duration of the war.

Repression and terror, as practised by the Soviet government against its own people, continued. In 1941 whole national groups, such as the German communities in the Volga region, were labelled as traitors and deported to remote parts of the USSR. Yet the need for labour reduced the numbers in the gulag by two-fifths between 1941 and 1944.

In addition to repression, propaganda was used to stir the Soviet people into action by appealing to the nationalism and patriotism of Soviet citizens. This was 'The Great Patriotic War' for Mother Russia. Traditional values were also used in giving concessions to the Orthodox Church. It collected money for the army and blessed troops before going into battle. This more liberal attitude by the government encouraged the belief that life would be easier after the war.

By the end of the war in 1945, the Soviet Union had emerged victorious but at an enormous cost. The war had resulted in the deaths of over twenty million Soviet citizens, the highest of any of the countries involved in the war. The human cost was also to be measured in the numbers of widows, orphans and invalids. The economic cost, too, was enormous, with over 25 million people left homeless and losses in factories and farms amounting to one-third of the country's wealth. Yet morale at the end of the war was high. The USSR emerged as the saviours of civilisation from Nazism and the regime deserved some of the credit for this. The war showed the regime's ability to mobilise the country's resources and also offered a justification for Stalin's pre-war policies.

LATE STALINISM 1945–53

At the end of the Second World War the Soviet people were exhausted from the effort required to defeat the German army. The war had come after the hardships endured in the campaign for industrialisation in the 1930s. By 1945 a large section of the Soviet people hoped for a relaxation in the tight government control which had been a central part of the Stalinist system. These hopes for change were to be disappointed. Stalin and the party leadership re-imposed pre-war policies, which strengthened their own positions as well as that of the Communist Party. The concessions given during the Second World War had clearly been measures of expediency rather than signs of a long-term relaxation of policy.

The party leadership was quick to reassert its authority through the use of terror and propaganda. The development of the Cold War was used as evidence of a continued foreign threat against which the Soviet population needed to be vigilant. 'Enemy elements' were rounded up and sent to the labour camps. Any signs of western influence were condemned and severely dealt with. This had a direct impact on all aspects of Soviet culture and led to the xenophobic campaign of the 'Zhdanovshchina' (a purge of cultural activity after 1945).

Rigid state control was reinforced over the war-shattered economy. The **fourth Five-Year Plan (1946–50)** aimed to restore the economy to pre-war levels, a massive undertaking in so short a time. The results were impressive. Industrial production recovered quickly, helped in a large part by the use of over two million slave labourers. Strong central planning by the government was an important factor in achieving such quick results. The **fifth Five-Year Plan (1951–55)** was less impressive as large amounts of resources were diverted into the building of grandiose projects, which had limited economic value. Overall, the performance of Soviet industry was impressive and from 1948 living standards in the towns started to recover, although conditions in the countryside were much slower to improve.

The concessions given to peasants during the war had weakened the collective farms and the power of the party in the countryside. The party leadership moved quickly to re-impose control over agriculture but agricultural production remained low and recovery was slow.

As the party's control over the economy was reasserted the leadership sought to strengthen its own position. In 1949 Stalin celebrated his seventieth birthday during which there was a wave of admiration. The cult of personality reached its peak in this period with the glorification of Stalin through paintings, sculptures and books. Yet Stalin's health had been in decline since the war and in this situation those around him were engaged in rivalry for power and influence. Immediately after the war the old guard of Stalin's associates, such as Molotov and Kaganovich, found themselves eclipsed by the rise of a younger generation within the party leadership. Among this new generation the chief rivals were Zhdanov, Malenkov and Beria. When Zhdanov died suddenly in 1948, Stalin brought Khrushchev back to Moscow from the Ukraine to be used as a counterweight against Malenkov and Beria. In 1953 there is evidence that Stalin was planning another major purge before he died. In January a group of doctors were arrested, accused of trying to assassinate the leadership. The 'Doctors' Plot' may have been the prelude to a campaign of terror against Soviet Jews but it was more likely to have been the first step towards the elimination of Beria and possibly other figures in the leadership. Stalin died before the purge could take place.

Stalin's power within the leadership had been in decline since 1945. He could no longer command his subordinates and he could maintain his position only through the use of intrigue. Although purges were more selective and limited after the war, the party leadership was still operating in an atmosphere of insecurity. The rivalry which developed within the leadership was also as much a result of the organisation of the Soviet State with its competing structures as it was a battle to succeed Stalin.

The period from 1945 to 1953 was marked by the reassertion of the power and control of the Soviet State and as a result there are few changes to be detected as pre-war policies were re-imposed. The desire for change, which had been present in a large section of society after the war, was ignored. The Stalinist system which had been developed in the 1930s became more entrenched. Future developments would show that for any change to occur the impetus would have to come from the leadership itself. Yet the regime was based on party structures which were keen to preserve their own status and in this sense the system proved increasingly inflexible when faced with the prospect of change.

KHRUSHCHEV AND DESTALINISATION 1953–64

When Stalin died in 1953 members of the Politburo formed a collective leadership. By 1956 Khrushchev had outmanoeuvred his main opponents, Malenkov and Beria. At the Twentieth Party Congress in 1956 Khrushchev felt confident enough to give a speech which criticised Stalin. He accused Stalin of developing a cult of personality, acting as a tyrant, using unnecessary terror and making economic mistakes. These criticisms glossed over the fact that the Politburo contained party members, including Khrushchev, who had risen through the ranks by implementing Stalin's policies.

For Khrushchev, the Soviet system needed to be rejuvenated by a return to the legality of Leninism. Khrushchev's reforms were to become known as destalinisation but Khrushchev was careful to ensure that attention was focused on Stalin and not the Soviet system itself.

Under Khrushchev there was a reduction in terror and some political prisoners were released. There was a reduction in the power of the party as economic decision-making was decentralised in an attempt to encourage more initiative and creativity in policy and therefore increase production. Yet in attempting to move away from rigid control by the party Khrushchev upset those who had most to gain from the continuation of the system developed by Stalin. The party apparatus reasserted its power and in 1964 Khrushchev was dismissed by the Politburo. The fact that a Soviet leader could be removed by a vote was, however, an indication that Khrushchev had made some changes to the system.

THE YEARS OF STABILITY 1964–85

Khrushchev's replacement as General Secretary was Leonid Brezhnev, a party man who was seen as a safe pair of hands. Brezhnev quickly reversed those aspects of destalinisation that had upset the party and there was even a limited recognition of the centenary of Stalin's birth in 1979. Yet there was no return to the widespread use of terror. In many cases Brezhnev continued destalinisation, for example in his more tolerant attitude to the Orthodox Church.

Brezhnev liked the trappings of power; he awarded himself numerous medals for rather dubious achievements, but he exercised less personal power than either Stalin or Khrushchev. He preferred to trust party comrades and let them get on with their jobs. The resulting stability made Brezhnev a popular leader but it also led to economic stagnation. The party structures, which had developed under Stalin, were now so entrenched that the system was difficult to change even if there was the will to do so. By the early 1980s the Soviet Union gave the impression of being a vast system grinding to a halt, much like the elderly Brezhnev who died in 1982.

Brezhnev's successor, Yuri Andropov, recognised the need for reform but he was too ill to follow through his ideas. When he died in 1984 the Politburo, in a desperate measure of self-preservation, elected the party bureaucrat Konstantin Chernenko as General Secretary. Chernenko was in his mid-seventies and was dying of emphysema when he was elected leader.

GORBACHEV AND THE END OF THE SOVIET UNION 1985–91

Chernenko's death in 1985 marked an end to an era of Soviet leaders from the generation that had risen through the ranks of the party during Stalin's leadership. With them went the last hopes of the Stalinist state. The new leader Mikhail Gorbachev was from a younger generation with a different outlook. He recognised that the whole Soviet system, which had become so entrenched, was performing poorly. Gorbachev made a serious and genuine attempt to rejuvenate the Soviet Union through his policies. The main elements were:

- *Perestroika.* A restructuring of the economy, which involved a measure of private enterprise to promote production, efficiency and higher quality goods.
- *Glasnost.* A policy of openness that encouraged the population to put forward new ideas and show initiative.
- *Democratisation.* An attempt to get more people involved in the Communist Party and political debate.

Gorbachev's reforms resulted in a more questioning approach to the Soviet system but ultimately led to a rejection of communism itself. In an attempt to bring about the first fundamental reform to the system built up by Stalin, Gorbachev unleashed forces which would completely destroy the Soviet Union. By the end of the 1980s a large proportion of the Soviet population were calling for an end to communist rule and the introduction of liberal democracy. In the republics, nationalist groups wanted a break-up of the Soviet state. By the end of 1991 the Soviet Union had ceased to exist. The system had become so entrenched it could not change without breaking.

A2 ASSESSMENT: THE SOVIET UNION AFTER LENIN 1924–41

HISTORIOGRAPHY

A consideration of different historical approaches to topics is an important skill for the student of history to develop. You may, like many students, find historiography difficult because it requires you to know the wider context of influences on historical writing which often fall outside the period you are directly studying. For example, interpretations of Stalin's policies in the 1930s have been influenced by events such as the Cold War and the fall of the Soviet Union, both of which occurred after the 1930s. Despite its challenges, historiography adds another level of understanding to studying topics, and an awareness both that historians differ in their views and that the way they approach the past is changing all the time. All this makes history especially exciting.

Writing extended answers on historiographical issues

As part of your assessment you will be required to write extended answers which are specifically geared to issues of historiography. These are different from standard essays in that an awareness of the range of relevant historiographical approaches is essential. If you write a standard answer to this type of question you will not meet the requirements of the question; for example, the question 'How and why have historians' interpretations of the causes of the Great Purges differed?' cannot be answered by writing a standard essay on the causes of the Great Purges. The key issues to address here are why and how **historians** have disagreed.

Writing historiographical essays usually requires you to explain the different perspectives and to assess their value.

Evaluating historical perspectives

It is useful to think of the following aspects when you read extracts from the works of historians:

- what is the main **thrust** of the source? (i.e. what is it saying?)
- what **evidence** is being used by the author to develop the argument? For example a speech by Stalin might be of more use to a historian approaching the study of the Soviet Union in the 1930s from the liberal intentionalist perspective, where the focus is on Stalin's leadership, than to a social historian wishing to focus on

developments in society. A collection of oral accounts by industrial workers would be more useful to a social historian.

- what **angle** does the author take? (i.e. does the author focus on one particular angle and neglect others?) It is worth remembering that two historians from the same school of history may look at the same issue from different angles.
- the **background** of the author (i.e. have the nationality, date and other background factors affected the way in which the author sees the issue?).
- the **perspective** of the author (i.e. which approach does the historian seem to be taking and to what school does the author belong? How have the underlying principles of this perspective affected the way in which the topic is approached?)

Explaining how historians agree/differ should be seen as a building block for moving on to consider why. This is what will usually be expected in high quality answers.

There are several pitfalls to avoid:

- Try to avoid an endless list of historians' names and their books. 'Name-dropping', in itself, is of limited use and examiners are well aware that students have often never read the books themselves but are merely regurgitating learnt lists of names. It is more important that you show an awareness of the views from different perspectives even if you have never read the books themselves and cannot even remember the names of historians involved. Showing an **understanding of the perspectives** is a higher level skill more likely to score marks.
- Take care in quoting from historians. A statement by a historian can be useful in summing up a relevant point or as illustrating a factor but they should be used sparingly. It is never advisable to use long quotations, especially in exam answers as the reward rarely compensates for the effort involved in learning the quote or the time taken to copy it out. Short, sharp quotes are preferable but think carefully about the purpose of the quotation. Just because a historian states something does not make it a fact. In other words, be careful not to confuse opinion with fact.
- Referring to different interpretations by historians can often result in a lapse into description rather than being used as a tool of analysis to develop your argument. For example, the answer that falls into outlining what historian A states and then goes on to what historian B states is not using the material effectively to raise it above the merely descriptive. It is much better to **state whether you agree or disagree with the perspectives** covered and **why**. Writing historiographical essays usually requires you to explain the different perspectives and to assess their value. Ensure that you evaluate the different approaches by relating each school of historians to their wider context and philosophical views. For example, consider the evidence they have used, the period they were writing in and the values which have influenced them. This will enable you to show your skills in evaluation and assessment and therefore gain more marks than a merely descriptive answer, however detailed.

History is a subject which by its very nature involves extensive reading, and in order to make maximum use of the material you have studied it is important to consider issues of historiography which are reflected in it. This will deepen your understanding of the topic to make you more competent as a historian.

AN EXAMPLE OF A HISTORIOGRAPHICAL QUESTION IN THE STYLE OF EDEXCEL

Study Sources A and E and answer the questions which follow.

Source A

While they did not have the same disastrous consequences in the case of industry as in that of agriculture, the same faults of (Stalin's) judgement reappear.

First, without any attempt to present a reasoned case, Stalin made a surprise appearance at the Council of Commissars and insisted that the figures which Gosplan (the State Planning Commission) proposed for the Five-Year Plan should be increased by up to – and in some cases over – 100 per cent.

Second . . . Stalin was obsessed with 'gigantomania'. He demanded industrial complexes to be built on a scale beyond Russia's resources to construct or operate. The result was that they either took far longer to complete than was economical, and then were constantly subject to breakdowns, or were left unfinished . . .

Third, Stalin's obsession with size was matched by his unrelenting insistence on haste. Not only did he throw the balance of the Five-Year Plan into chaos by doubling the target figures . . . but he then demanded that it should be carried out in four, not five years.

Finally, confronted by the failure to meet impossible dates and targets, Stalin denounced those responsible as guilty of sabotage, wrecking and conspiracy, attacking in particular the former bourgeois and foreign specialists who provided him with convenient scapegoats, but on whom Soviet industry was heavily dependent for technical and managerial expertise.

. . . (Stalin's) revolution from above was not the replacement of a capitalist by a socialist economy, but something which has become much more familiar since: using the power of the state to launch an assault on a backward society . . . Yet, for all its shortcomings, centralisation had the same decisive advantage for Stalin of allowing him to keep control, to intervene . . . and to get a grip on situations which were out of control.

From A. Bullock, *Hitler and Stalin: Parallel Lives* (1991).

Source B

Both before and after its introduction in 1929, the First Five-Year Plan went through many versions and revisions, with competing sets of planners responding in different degrees to pressures from the politicians.

Industry was exhorted to 'overfulfil' the Plan rather than simply to carry it out. The Plan, in other words, was not meant to allocate resources or balance demands but to drive the economy forward pell-mell . . . Supply priorities were not determined by the written Plan but by a series of *ad hoc* decisions from the Commissariat of Heavy Industry, the government's Council of Labour and Defence, and even the party's politburo.

But the top priorities were constantly changing in response to crisis, impending disaster, or a new raising of targets in one of the key industrial sectors . . . The successful Soviet manager during the First Five-Year Plan was less like an obedient functionary than a wheeling-and-dealing entrepreneur, ready to cut corners and seize any opportunity to outdo his competitors.

The party organisations of Ukraine and the Urals were at daggers drawn over the distribution of investment monies for mining and metallurgical complexes and machine-building complexes . . . Intense rivalries also sprang up over the location of specific plants scheduled for construction during the First Five-Year Plan . . . A similar battle had raged from 1926 over the site of the Urals Machine-Building Plant: Sverdlovsk, the ultimate victor, began construction on local funds and without central authorisation in order to force Moscow's hand on the location decision.

Strong regional competition often resulted in a double victory – the authorisation of two separate plants, one in each region, where the planners' original intention had been to build only a single plant. This was one factor behind the soaring targets and ever-increasing costs . . . But it was not the only factor, for Moscow's central politicians and planners were clearly in the grip of 'gigantomania', the obsession with hugeness. The Soviet Union must build more and produce more than any other country.

From Sheila Fitzpatrick, *The Russian Revolution* (1994).

Source C

During a trip from Kiev to Moscow in 1939, my chauffeur told me that the tyres which were being issued for our cars were wearing out much too quickly. In fact, they were blowing out at the sides while they were still almost brand new. When I got to Moscow, I told Stalin that this manufacturing defect was costing a lot of time and money: Stalin never liked to hear anyone criticise something that was Soviet-made. He listened to my complaint with obvious displeasure. Then he angrily instructed me to liquidate this situation and to find the culprits . . .

When I reported to Stalin, I stressed that we were producing poor-quality tyres because, in our desire to economise, we had violated the production procedure recommended by the firm from which the equipment was purchased . . . The tyre workers may have surpassed their quota, but they have overdone it. Our workers should have paid more attention to quality when applying the tyre cording. All the shock-workers on the honour board at the factory were, in actual fact, ruining what they produced . . .

From N. Khrushchev, *Khrushchev Remembers* (1971).

Source D
Whatever the validity of certain official claims, it remains true beyond question that the second Five-Year Plan period was one of impressive achievement, as is clear from the commodity statistics . . .

Both in volume and in degree of sophistication the advances recorded in these years did help to transform the whole balance of industry and to diminish very substantially the USSR's dependence on foreign countries for its capital goods.

From A. Nove, *An Economic History of the USSR 1917–91* (1992).

Source E
Any overall judgement of the first three Five-Year Plans is of necessity a complicated and controversial matter . . . The plans did succeed – and succeed strikingly – in developing industry . . .

Yet the cost was tremendous. Soviet authorities could accomplish their aims only by imposing great hardships on the people and by mobilising the country in a quasi-military manner for a supreme effort.

From N. Riasanovsky, *A History of Russia* (1993).

Question 1
a) Using the evidence in Sources A and B and your own knowledge, consider Stalin's responsibility for the chaos which occurred during the implementation of the First Five-Year Plan?
b) 'Despite its human cost, the Five-Year Plans had resulted in the economic modernisation of the Soviet Union by 1941'.
   Using the evidence of Sources A, B, C, D and E and your own knowledge, explain how far you agree with this opinion.

How you should answer these questions

Question (a): This question is designed to test your ability to reach a reasoned judgement on a historical issue, based on an evaluation of historical perspectives, and through the use of sources and own knowledge.

Sources A and B give two different opinions on the role of Stalin based not only on the points stated but also by the general approach and perspective taken by the two historians. They represent part of the wider debate on the importance of Stalin in the course of historical change. These points should be considered in your answer.

Mark scheme

LEVEL 1: simple statements based predominantly on the sources OR own knowledge.

LEVEL 2: developed statements making use of both the sources and own knowledge to present a judgement. There will be some awareness of the different perspectives taken by the authors of the sources and different schools of historians. The answer will, however, probably be unbalanced.

LEVEL 3: developed and sustained explanation which shows confident use and evaluation of the sources and different historical perspectives. There will be a secure integration of sources and own knowledge to present a reasoned argument in response to the question.

Worked example: student's answer and examiner's comments

Historians have argued over the degree of responsibility attached to Stalin for the chaotic implementation of the Five-Year Plan. The sources show two different views. In Source A Bullock lays the blame for the chaos caused during the First Five-Year Plan on Stalin, whereas Fitzpatrick seems to stress a broader range of factors.

Bullock comments on Stalin's lack of 'judgement' and 'obsession' with 'gigantomania'. 'Obsession' is mentioned again in reference to his insistence on haste. Clearly, according to Bullock the Five-Year Plan was thrown into chaos because of Stalin's actions which Bullock seems to be suggesting were those of an unbalanced man. This emphasis on the role of the individual, namely Stalin, is typical of the western intentional viewpoint which sees individuals as important in the process of driving historical change. To this school Stalin represents a dictator controlling events for his own purposes. Fitzpatrick agrees that the government headed by Stalin was 'in the grip of 'gigantomania', the obsession with hugeness' but in contrast, the causes of the chaos are not so simple. Fitzpatrick mentions the inter-party rivalry, which led to disruption and resulted in 'ad hoc decisions'. The rivalry between the Ukraine and the Urals is given as an example and the comment that building took place 'without central authorisation' contrasts with that of Bullock who sees Stalin guiding events much more strongly. Fitzpatrick seems to be making more use of the local sources available to historians since 'Glasnost' and as a result her approach focuses on the implementation of the Plan at local level rather than the centre (Bullock). The conclusions Fitzpatrick draws are similar to those of the structuralist school which stress the structural make-up of the Soviet Union as a cause of chaos which generally limited orders issued by the government and in some cases actually pushed the government into taking action.

Thus, despite some small agreements these two historians differ in their views because they are examining the issue from different standpoints; Bullock focusing on the role of Stalin and the 'revolution from above', whilst Fitzpatrick examines events from 'below'. Both of these perspectives are useful in explaining the chaos of the First Five-Year Plan as they examine the issue from different angles using different evidence. The intentionalists focus on Stalin and make use of his speeches as evidence of his intentions. On the other hand the structuralists and social historians use evidence from groups within the Party and society as a whole to check whether Stalin's orders were carried out, changed or even ignored at local level. Stalin was highly skilled at ensuring he aligned himself with the views of rank and file party members and used them to his own advantage. Thus, it is reasonable to suggest that although Stalin may not have been able to completely control events he was capable of using the chaos during this period to strengthen his own position against those who threatened his power both within and outside the Party. In this sense Stalin does bear a lot of the responsibility for the chaos which accompanied industrialisation.

This is a thoughtful answer, which uses the sources to develop points of disagreement and agreement between the two historians. Both historians are related to their wider perspective and some good points are made concerning their differing approaches to the same issue. Areas of agreement could have been examined more, especially the implied references to the purges and their effects on industrial development.

Own knowledge is included to develop the points made about the two sources, but the opportunity to examine other approaches more fully is not taken. A judgement is made with the reasoning provided. This is a sound, if rather unbalanced, answer which offers an evaluation of the sources and includes some material from own knowledge. It would be marked at Level 2.

Question (b): This question requires an extended answer which can show your ability to explain and evaluate differing interpretations of a historical issue.

Mark scheme
LEVEL 1: able to describe different interpretations of historical issues to show an awareness of how they differ. There is likely to be a reliance on the sources.
LEVEL 2: shows an awareness of different historical interpretations by reference to sources and own knowledge. There will be **some explanation** of these differences based on their use of evidence.
LEVEL 3: shows an awareness of the wider debate which the sources illustrate and how the different historical interpretations relate to the concerns, attitudes and values

of the historians involved at the time of writing. There is an **evaluation** of the interpretations and a judgement based on this evaluation. The judgement may not be developed or sustained.

LEVEL 4: able to provide an explanation and **full evaluation** of different historical interpretations by integrating evidence from the sources with own knowledge. Able to assess the relative value of different perspectives to make a reasoned, independent judgement about the inter-relationship between historians and the issues they are studying.

The sources can be used to illustrate a range of different viewpoints but should also be seen as relating to different historical approaches within the wider debate on Stalin's economic achievements. Sources A and B can be used to develop the intentionalist/revisionist debate, Source D is from the perspective of an economic historian, Source E relates to the debate over the range of alternatives. Source C illustrates one aspect of Soviet historiography and can be used to discuss the changes in Soviet historiography since Stalin.

BIBLIOGRAPHY

There is a wide range of books available for the study of Stalin and the Soviet Union. The following would be particularly useful for AS Level students and as a general introduction to A2 Level:

G. Freeze (ed), *Russia: a History* (OUP 1997)
G. Hosking, *A History of the Soviet Union* (Fontana 1992)
G. Hughes & S. Welfare, *Red Empire* (Weidenfeld & Nicolson 1990)
J. Scott, *Behind the Urals: an American Worker in Russia's City of Steel* (Indiana University Press, 1942)
J. M. Thompson, *Russia and the Soviet Union* (Westview 1990)
J. N. Westwood, *Endurance and Endeavour* (OUP 1981)

The following would be particularly useful for A2 Level and more detailed research:

S. Alliluyeva, *Twenty Letters to a Friend* (Hutchinson 1967)
G. Boffa, *The Stalin Phenomenon* (Cornell 1982)
A. Bullock, *Hitler and Stalin: Parallel Lives* (Harper Collins 1991)
E. H. Carr, *The Russian Revolution from Lenin to Stalin 1917–29* (Macmillan 1979)
R. Davies, *History in the Gorbachev Revolution* (Macmillan 1989)
S. Fitzpatrick, *The Russian Revolution* (Opus 1994)
G. Gill, *Stalinism* (Macmillan 1990)
M. McCauley, *The Soviet Union* (Longman 1993)
J. Laver, *Joseph Stalin: from Revolutionary to Despot* (Hodder & Stoughton 1993)
J. Milner, *Russian Revolutionary Art* (Oresko 1979)
A. Nove, *An Economic History of the USSR* (Penguin 1992)
R. Service, *A History of Twentieth Century Russia* (Penguin 1997)
R. Stites, *Russian Popular Culture: Entertainment and Society Since 1900* (Cambridge University Press 1992)

D. Volkogonov, *Stalin: Triumph and Tragedy* (Harper Collins 1990)

D. Volkogonov, *Trotsky: the Eternal Revolutionary* (Harper Collins 1996)

D. Volkogonov, *The Rise and Fall of the Soviet Empire* (Harper Collins 1998)

C. Ward, *Stalin's Russia* (Edward Arnold 1993)

Useful works of fiction for this period include:

A. Koestler, *Darkness at Noon* (Vintage 1940)

G. Orwell, *Animal Farm* (Penguin 1945)

G. Orwell, *1984* (Penguin 1949)

B. Pasternak, *Doctor Zhivago* (Collins 1958)

A. Solzhenitsyn, *One Day in the Life of Ivan Denisovich* (Penguin 1962)

The following websites contain material related to a study of Stalin:

http://www.marxists.org/archive/lenin/index.htm
(Contains archive of material by Lenin)

http://www.marxists.org/archive/marx/index.htm
(Contains archive of Marx's works)

http://www.marxists.org/reference/archive/stalin/index.htm
(Contains archive of Stalin's works)

http://mars.acnet.wnec.edu/~grempelcourses/russia/lectures/
33stalintrot.html (Contains article on the struggle
between Stalin and Trotsky)

http://www.anu.edu.au/polsci/marx/classics/trotsky.html
(Archive of Trotsky's works)

http://www.fbuch.com/leon.htm (Information on Trotsky)

http://hsc.csu.edu.au/modhist/courses/2unit/twencent/russia
(Articles on Stalin and the Russian Revolution)

http://www.fordham.edu/halsall/mod/modsbook39.html
(Contains sources on Stalin)